The Cyclist's Body Book

Frank Westell and Simon Martin

The Cyclist's Body Book

Springfield Books Limited

© Frank Westell and Simon Martin

This edition first published 1991 by Springfield Books Limited, Norman Road, Denby Dale, Huddersfield HD8 8TH West Yorkshire, England

First edition 1991

British Library Cataloguing in Publication Data
Westell, Frank
    The Cyclist's Body Book
    1 Physical fitness. Cycling
    I Title II Martin, Simon
    613.71

ISBN 0 947655 24 7

Acknowledgements

The authors and publishers wish to acknowledge the help of the following people:

The British Cycling Federation, for the UCI's list of banned substances.

Dr Chris Jarvis, for his help with the medical aspects of the text.

Peter Keen, for the use of his work on Four Levels of Training Intensity in chapter 2.

Steve Livingstone, for helping with the pictures for the stretching and massage sections.

The Sports Council, for the warning about banned substances in herbal preparations which appears on page 141.

I also wish to acknowledge the help of Katie Edwards and her nimble fingers at the word processor, and Frank Rasey and Murray Graham for assisting my observations of the ageing cyclist.
FW

Photographic credits

George Smith (pages 39, 40, 43, 44, 45 and 46)

Graham Watson (frontis and pages 8, 18, 32, 68, 88, 95, 98, 130 and the cover photographs)

Cover design: Chris Hand
Inset design: Douglas Martin Associates
Illustrations: Barry Davies
Typesetting: Armitage Typo/Graphics Ltd, Huddersfield
Printed and bound in Great Britain by The Bath Press

DEDICATED TO THE MEMORY OF EDNA RAYNE,
A LIFE-LONG KEEN CYCLIST, WHO ENCOURAGED ME TO WRITE THIS BOOK,
AND CONSTANTLY URGED ME TO 'KEEP IT SIMPLE'.
FW

Contents

1 Let's keep you on the road

Every year more people take up cycling. We caught the bug many years ago, and in that time have seen and heard of several cyclists having to give up their sport due to health problems that could have been dealt with − if only they'd known how.

There is no problem finding a book to tell you what to do if your bike is damaged or in poor repair, but you have got to look long and hard to find one that covers what you, the rider, need to do if you are unfit, injured or ill. This book aims to do just that.

Knowing bike riders, we're resigned to the fact that one book cannot possibly deal with everything that might happen to you but as we've covered all the important health and fitness problems encountered by a sporting cyclist at one time or another, you will be able to use this book to help yourself to many years of successful cycling.

The foundation: how the body works

Why do we train? Obviously, to get fit. But what does that mean? In training we are trying to get the body and mind used to performing better: riding faster, for longer, recovering more quickly and staying out of injury and illness. Training improves the efficiency of the body's various systems − muscles, lungs, heart and so on − so that gradually they are able to work to higher standards.

The problem that most cyclists have is that they don't know *why* they do what they do. They'll adopt a training routine that the current big winner follows, or they'll fit in with what everybody else is doing or − most likely − they'll do what they feel like doing.

Fair enough: we'd all rather be out doing it than reading about it, but the cyclists who choose to stay in the dark about training and − more specifically − the changes that they are causing in their bodies, will never reach their full potential.

You can get as scientific as you like with this stuff, but it does not have to be heavy. Our object in this book is to keep you on the road and help you to get more out of bike-riding. Simply put, it's more fun to be able to ride fast and recover quickly, than it is to be a permanently exhausted plodder.

If you don't know what your body needs and what your particular brand of training is achieving, there's a good chance that you are actually wasting time and energy. You may even be riding into injury and early retirement. Learn just a little about training and physiology and it will give you gigantic returns.

To understand the how and why of training, let's briefly look at how the body works when you're on your bike.

Getting energy

To work, muscles require energy. We obtain this from some of the food we eat in the form of *glycogen*. Some glycogen is kept in the muscles for immediate use but most is stored in the liver. Just as when a car uses petrol, waste products are given off which have to be expelled as exhaust fumes or the engine will clog up and stop, so it is with the human 'engine'. When the body uses energy, waste products are left behind which, if not removed from the muscles, would clog them up. To fuel the muscular contractions which get you down the road, and to break down these waste products, the body uses oxygen, pulled in via the **lungs**. In fact, the lungs perform several functions: they obtain and supply air; they remove waste products such as carbon dioxide, and they get rid of excess heat and water.

Train your lungs

As a sporting cyclist, you are not in the happy position of top-class 100-metre runners, who may be able to complete their events while holding their breath. Instead, your performance depends on your lung power: specifically, on how much carbon dioxide and water you can 'blow off' and how much oxygen you can pull in. Your lungs, just like your muscles, also respond to training. ('Air', by the way, is not all oxygen. In fact, only about 20 per cent of the air we breathe is oxygen, and part of the training process is to help you be able to extract more of it.)

The lungs are made up of millions of little air sacs called *alveoli*: around 600 million of them. When we breathe in, we draw air through the mouth and nose. It then travels through increasingly smaller and smaller airways to the alveoli. In exercise nearly 80 per cent of oxygen intake is through the mouth.

The average male has a total lung capacity of approximately 6 litres. If he were to breathe all the way out he would still have around 1.2 litres of air (his *residual volume*) left in his lungs. The difference (4.8 litres) is what is known as your 'vital capacity', which is usually 4-5 litres for men and 3-4 litres for women. It's an important measurement because it lets you know how much air you can process, and your ability to get oxygen to your muscles is one of the major factors in how well you can perform.

A cyclist of a good standard usually has a vital capacity in the region of 6-7 litres, and a talented few can raise their vital capacity to more than 8 litres. Although your potential vital capacity is predetermined genetically, you can make sure you push it to its limits if you work hard and progressively during childhood and adolescence. If you haven't had a very active childhood, then you may find your efforts to improve lung power later in life are not that rewarding. The importance of early conditioning – whether it happens naturally through play or is enforced by circumstances – was first brought to the world's attention when African runners began to dominate athletics. Although conventionally under-prepared, many of them, it turned out, had run 10 or 20 miles a day to school and back throughout childhood.

Along with your vital capacity, which you will train with quality steady state riding – not just hours of 'plodding' – you can also improve your riding by increasing the strength and flexibility of your respiratory muscles, especially the *diaphragm*, a sheet of muscular membrane that divides the inside of the chest from the abdominal cavity, and the intercostals, the 'washboard' muscles between your ribs.

When it comes to 'blowing off' waste products, a cyclist of good standard should be able to expel more than 80 per cent of his lung's functional capacity in one second. This determines what is known as your *maximum minute ventilation*, important because it is not so much the amount of oxygen you can *load*, but how much carbon dioxide you can *unload*, that counts in high-level competition. That painful, distressing point at which you can't deliver oxygen and release carbon dioxide fast enough to maintain energy levels is called your anaerobic threshold (known to cyclists as 'blowing up').

Blood for transport

Another part of the picture is the transport system needed to deliver oxygen and glycogen to the muscles and to remove waste. This is your blood, which contains plasma to deliver energy material and red cells to deliver oxygen and to remove carbon dioxide, excess heat and excess water. The transport network is a system of arteries, along which the blood delivers energy material and oxygen, and veins, along which it removes waste products.

The engine driving the blood around is the body's pump – actually two pumps connected together – the **heart**. The heart collects the blood containing waste products from the muscles and pumps it to the lungs. There the waste products are removed and replaced by oxygen. The heart then collects the blood again, this time from the lungs, and pumps it back to the muscles. Some blood is also sent to the liver to collect more energy materials. In this way there is a continuous supply of energy material and of oxygen, and a continuous removal of waste products so that they do not clog the muscles.

During heavy exercise 60 per cent of the heart's output (determined by heart rate and volume of blood pumped per minute) goes to the muscles of the body, compared with 4 per cent at rest. A normal heart at rest may pump 4 litres of blood per minute. The heart of a working top cyclist may be pumping 30 litres per minute.

Muscles: you and your twitches

During exercise, muscles cause the actual body movements. Muscles consist of thousands of long, hair-like fibres bound together in bundles. These are attached at each end to bones: when the muscles contract they shorten and pull the bones, moving parts of the body. Muscles do only two things: they contract or relax. A muscle does not 'lengthen' or stretch itself; this is only done by other muscles or by gravity.

To meet the wide-ranging demands of different activities – fast or slow, strong or gentle, short bursts or constant activity – we have different kinds of muscle fibres. All are represented through the three basic types of muscle fibres classified as slow-twitch oxidative (SO) fibre; intermediate fast-twitch oxidative-glycolytic (FOG) fibre; fast-twitch glycolytic (FG) fibre.

Although we have the three types of fibres, we usually train to develop either the slow- or fast- twitch by specific training sessions, so we'll only refer to those two types. Slow-twitch fibres are endurance muscles. They are aerobic; they depend on oxygen to work. Fast-twitch fibres give you power and speed. They are anaerobic; they are not dependent on oxygen for their energy supply. The proportion of slow-twitch to fast-twitch largely decides what you are good at. Leg muscles that are predominantly fast-twitch, for example, are just what you need for sprinting, but probably won't do you much good on a long hilly road race.

With the right type of training you can make the most of what you've got, but you're not going to change your basic proportions, which are mostly inherited.

Cycling, being an endurance sport, mainly uses and develops slow-twitch muscle fibres. Steady state riding – riding at a steady, even pace – uses mostly slow-twitch fibres and so will develop these, and to some extent, the fast-twitch fibres as well.

Fast-twitch fibres come into play when power and speed are called for. Interval training will help to develop both types of fast-twitch fibres, if the effort periods are structured correctly. As you're not going to change your genetic make-up, is there any point in trying to train these various types of muscles? Yes, there is. While the number of slow- or fast-twitch fibres does not change during endurance training, you will get a general development to each of the fibres, particularly the slow-twitch – which will give you increased aerobic potential.

Through progressive endurance training, you will train your muscles to become more efficient in oxidizing glucose and fats; they will create less lactic acid and you will be able to train and race harder and longer without being stopped by tired legs – or 'local muscular fatigue', as it's known! Also you may gain as much as an 80 per cent increase of myoglobin, the oxygen-carrying protein pigment in muscle, which will make more oxygen consistently available to the muscle cells. That's essential for handling the aerobic workload of an endurance sport. During the sustained aerobic – literally 'with oxygen' – effort of getting in the miles, the ability to mobilize and oxidize fat is increased, so the percentage of fat used as an energy source develops in relation to the period of the endurance training session.

Although steady state riding is an important factor in your preparation, some people take it too far. Most bike-riders seem obsessed with it. Let's face it, it's just so much easier to go out for a steady ride than to put yourself on the rack of sustained bursts of high-intensity speed work. But if you're going to reach your full potential, you must include high-intensity training in the later stages of your preparation.

Let's look at the other links in the performance chain – the links you are strengthening and making more efficient by training.

The specifics: how training improves the way the body works

There's nothing quite like the shock of race pace, even if you think you've trained hard. What's going on? To do extra work, such as in a race, muscles demand more energy materials and more oxygen. This means that the heart has to pump more blood per minute to get them there. It does this both by squeezing out more blood per beat and by increasing the number of beats. If the heart is not used to supplying this extra blood it will not be able to squeeze out very much more per beat. The only alternative is for it to beat faster and faster. The catch is that there is a limit to how fast it can do this and still perform efficiently.

When the heartbeat gets over about 180 per minute, the time available for the heart to refill with blood before it has to pump it all out again is so small that it cannot do it completely. As a result, waste products aren't completely removed, and oxygen and glycogen don't get through to the muscles. You come to a grinding halt.

However, the heart is a muscle, albeit a special type of muscle, and you can develop it like any other muscle. Being an endurance activity, cycling will develop the thickness of the cardiac muscle of the left side of the heart, producing greater power to push out more blood to meet the increased need of the body. If, by regular hard training, you repeatedly ask the heart to pump more blood, you will stimulate it to increase the size of its chambers so that it can take in more blood each time it beats; then it does not need to beat as fast.

As you get fitter, you will find you have to work harder and harder to get your pulse rate up into the 180 beats per minute range. This adaptation is known as the 'training effect' and is one of the prime reasons for training. Cycling, being such an endurance exercise, is probably the best way to improve the heart muscle. It strengthens the muscle fibres of the heart and as a result makes it more efficient.

To support this improved muscle there must be improved circulation to the heart itself. We call this *collateral circulation* – the formation of new blood vessels and the dilation, or expansion, of existing vessels to improve the blood flow to the muscle fibres of the heart. With the development of the collateral system, there is an actual increase in the supply of blood to the heart itself.

You will develop your heart in different ways according to the type of training you do. Steady basic fitness riding (getting the miles in), during which your pulse rate is mainly around sub-120 beats per minute will, as your fitness improves, increase the size of the heart's chambers. You can monitor this progress during your steady state training period by recording your pulse rate daily. You should find that as you feel fitter your pulse will become slower.

This is a good sign, but not important on its own. There is little point in having a big chamber of anything unless you are also able to fill it and pump it out when needed. That's why you need to alter the emphasis in your training and develop 'the pump'. This is done by introducing – and progressively increasing – high intensity training, training that takes your pulse rate over 120 beats per minute.

Do this and you will increase the output of blood with each heart beat. Since the heart is a volume organ, its size and capacity are very important. The better the volume capacity, the better the stroke volume and cardiac output with each beat.

High intensity training includes speed, interval and all high-speed efforts. Heart rate is increased to well past 120 beats per minute (adjusted according to your age). This can also be monitored by the strength of the pulse when making your daily record. The ideal for a racing cyclist is a slow, strong pulse.

You will also get a peripheral benefit from cardiovascular training. This means that you will develop more collateral vessels in other muscles of the body, giving you reserve capacity and increasing the overall efficiency of your cardiovascular system.

Training has a similar effect on the lungs: there is a limit to how fast we can breathe and still do so effectively. Hard training improves the efficiency of the lungs so that the muscles' demands for oxygen, and the need for the removal of waste products, can be met at a slower rate of breathing. With regular training you can even slightly increase the volume of blood in your body, so you can increase the amounts of glycogen and oxygen you can shift, increasing the body's efficiency even more.

A 'training effect' also takes place within the muscles: they become more efficient at using the materials supplied to them by the heart and lungs. If muscles are not used to regular hard work, many of the fibres fall into disuse and become under-developed. Hard training increases the number of fibres available for work, so improving the efficiency of the whole muscle.

In addition, the number of arteries and veins will increase. This, together with the increase in blood volume, means that the supply of energy is improved: the muscles not only work at a higher standard, but can also keep going longer.

Body weight and metabolism are also targets for training areas. Your overall body weight is actually less important than how much body fat you have compared to lean body mass (muscle). Ideally, only 10 − 15 per cent of your weight should be body fat; this gives you a high power to weight ratio. Most sedentary Western men have 25 to 30 per cent of their weight as body fat. Cycle training helps by reducing the percentage of total body fat. In general, the more unfit and untrained the individual, the greater his percentage of total body fat.

Bone metabolism is also improved with training, which increases both bone density and bone strength. Training increases the number of oxygen-carrying components of the blood, the red blood cells, and there are benefits to the glands as well. Training improves the metabolism of certain adrenalin-like substances, known as *endorphins*, which tend to waste the body's oxygen supply. There may also be a connection between endorphins and your emotional state: fit persons have less of a tendency toward depression and in general are happier than the unfit.

The key thing to remember about training − if you want to continue to improve − is that it's no good repeating the same training runs over and again. If you keep the amount of work done at each training session at a reasonably constant level, then the efficiency of your heart, lungs, muscles and so on will soon reach that level and stick − with no further improvement in your performance. Instead, you must gradually increase the intensity and the duration of training. It's a basic principle, but one that is often forgotten. It's not just a case of 'doing the miles', for guess what? If your training is consistently moderate, that's just what your standard in racing will be.

Checklist

All racing cyclists should keep the following:

1 Personal file − personal details.

2 Personal results − details of races and places. If you don't finish, state reasons.

3 Training diary − this must be made out every day. Record pulse rate, training, weather, training partners, and comments on own fitness. By keeping these details you and your coach can decide future races and training.

Principles of conditioning

Conditioning is the specific adaptation to the demands of your sport. The principles are very appropriate to cyclists, as they are based on the overload principle of gradually increasing the strenuousness of a training routine.

1. Warm up and warm down − often neglected but a very important principle. By warming up, you prepare your body for the effort ahead; this will help you to avoid injury and enable you to get better results from your efforts. The warm down is equally important, as it is not good for your system to be working at maximum or sub maximum effort and then suddenly to stop.

2. Routine − well before the season starts, set up a daily routine of exercise and stretching. Most people are happy to set up a training programme but seem reluctant to include a stretching session. It is often only a half-hearted effort. By planning a routine of general exercise and stretching you will get more from your training.

3. Gradualness − ensure that all your physical efforts are gradually increased.

4. Timing − by creating a timetable of all your daily activities you can bring balance to your training. Consider all the work that you do − business, domestic and social − to prevent overdoing it. We are more prone to injury when tired.

5. Intensity − as your training increases and your fitness improves so should the intensity of your effort. Progressive increase in intensity is the key to improved performance. We often make the mistake of prolonging the training session rather than increasing the tempo or work load.

6. Capacity level − self-assessment is required here. In order to work to your true capacity, you must assess your physiological limits so that you

can work as closely to them as health and safety factors will allow. You must seek to work to **your** levels, not anybody else's.

7. Strength – strength is important in all sport but particularly in cycle racing. Strength should be developed for greater speed and endurance.

8. Motivation – the personal coach is a great asset in the motivation of a racing cyclist. But in the absence of a coach it is possible to develop the techniques of self-motivation. Set clear, precise, specific goals that can be achieved – people to beat, times to smash, races to win, medals to win – all play a part in motivation. Think positive and create the feeling of 'I'm a winner'.

9. Specialisation – training should consist of endurance, strength, speed, flexibility and relaxation geared to your chosen specific area of the sport. Do not specialise too early, if you are new to the sport – try all its facets, then assess your general strengths and weaknesses and choose the specific area in which you wish to excel.

10. Relaxation – relaxation is too often under-rated. We take it for granted and think we know how to do it or have a right to it. We do not. It is an art or technique that we need to work at to develop. It is essential to life and even more to sport, for it will ease tension and fatigue, and aid recovery from your training efforts. As with most things, practice makes perfect; practise this area of your preparation and you will be well rewarded.

2 Training

As we get more involved in cycle racing, we usually settle on a pattern of training. This pattern is affected by the area in which we live, the club we belong to, races that we compete in, the people we like to train with, plus social, domestic and business commitments.

Organised riders will work out a progressive development plan, plotting performance objectives to be achieved each year; physical and psychological development, including technical preparation and tactical skills, all leading to ultimate goals. The other end of the scale is, unfortunately, typical of the majority of riders, even those who really would like to 'get somewhere'. They do much the same form of training and racing year in year out, with training sessions determined by how they feel as they go out of the door or, even worse, by the whims of their training companions. By presenting an alternative, we hope to make it easy to convert to a more organised approach.

Know what you want

Your planned objectives will depend on your level of commitment to cycle racing, your present state of fitness and the time you have available for training. But what will really get you out of the door is having a goal to chase – something that inspires you. Spend some time, now, thinking about what you want to achieve. If you don't know, however roughly, where you are going, then you're not going to get there – and you won't have a clue about what sort of training you should be doing.

Write down your specific goals. Be as specific and precise as you can be. 'To get fit' sounds a worthy aim, but it's not exactly motivational. It's too vague. How fit? How will you know when you've achieved it? 'Fit enough to complete' – a specific race or training session – you choose! – in a specific time, is more likely to get you out of the door on a cold, wet night. It also has the advantage that you know whether you are getting near to your target. If you're not on course you can adjust your training accordingly. And you'll know when you reach it.

With some objectives in mind, your next step is to make a personal assessment. This is a current reality check, so be honest! You know what you want to achieve; now your aim is to find out what resources you've got behind you. The more honest and thorough you are with this assessment, the more effective your training programme, because your race preparation will grow out of the gap between what you want to achieve and where you are starting from.

Spend some time thinking about this, then commit it to paper. Once you have written it down you can check and re-check progress made.

Reality check

* List your physical strengths and weaknesses. What is your present standard of fitness? Do you need to be stronger, faster or have more stamina? What is your current state of health? Are you prone to injury and/or illness?

* List what places you have achieved or times you have done.

* Think back over your worst ever performance. What made it so disastrous? What went wrong? What, if anything, makes you a DNF or DNS?

* Now do the same for your most successful event. What went right? Are there obvious differences in your pattern of preparation, or in what your goals were?

* List your mental attitudes to training, races and other competitors. Write down what psychological skills you need to develop.

* List your mechanical needs and technical shortcomings. Is your equipment in first-class condition (do not confuse this with 'is it new')?

* Check all your equipment and list areas to be dealt with, in order of importance. Get someone to check your riding position when riding steady, and also under effort. Be honest about your technical abilities: do you feel comfortable riding wheel to wheel? Can you corner effectively? Do you know how to ride in echelon?

* Finally, list your tactical abilities, or lack of. Writing out your personal physical, psychological, technical and tactical assessment will help you to focus on what needs to be worked on in the coming months.

Planning your training

We all have problems with time − there is never enough of it. Training needs to be planned to fit in with other activities that also need some of your precious time.

Make a realistic assessment of the time that you have available for training each week throughout the year, for − make no mistake − training is an all year round activity. Once you have decided the training time that you have per week, use that time only for health and fitness development. We will discuss later how this time can be effectively used in differing situations.

However, don't fall into the trap of being inflexible in your training routine. There may be other unplanned calls on your time. As the year goes on there can be setbacks – or what appear to be setbacks. You might be selected to go on an international race, or your family might 'select' you to go on holiday, which means you are away from your normal training routine and environment.

In such circumstances it is not unknown for riders to 'talk themselves unfit' – they'll persuade themselves that they are losing fitness because they are not following their set programme of so many laps of a given road circuit. Be aware all the time of what a particular exercise – be it racing or training – is doing for you, even though it may take place in different surroundings. The opposite can also happen; riders on long international trips such as the world championships, Olympic or Commonwealth Games have a tendency to feel that the atmosphere of the occasion will miraculously keep them fit without their having to throw a leg over a saddle.

So once you have mapped out your training plan, be prepared to modify it to take care of unexpected racing trips, illness, or whatever comes up.

The four training stages

The training year can be split up into four stages:

1. Basic
2. Intensity/Racing
3. Intensity/Peak
4. Recovery

Each represents the important phases required for your physiological and psychological conditioning. Ideally the transition through the stages should be a smooth flow, with one training level naturally preparing you for and leading you to the next stage.

1 *Basic stage (16-20 weeks)*

The basic stage is predominantly aerobic development – riding 'with oxygen' – through long steady distance (LSD) riding. (*See* **Train your lungs** *page 10.*) It is the cornerstone of your training.
Note: LSD traditionally stands for long slow distance; our experience is that most riders put the emphasis too much on the slow – we believe it should stand for long steady distance.

This basic aerobic training, building up stamina, will develop all the body systems. It is measured in hours spent in the saddle, the eventual duration depending on the amount of time normally spent racing.

The further you expect to race, the longer the LSD sessions should become. Important as a basis for a programme, LSD can be done alone or in a group. Company is an advantage, because conversation helps to relieve the monotony. You can start with 30-minute rides if you are a real beginner, and go up to the high levels of professional and international amateur riders, who might be in the saddle for as long as six hours. Gears should be low to medium, allowing you to pedal at optimum revs but comfortably, and to keep up a steady effort.

Gradually increase the time you are spending on the road. As time goes on not only does the distance increase, but so does the speed because of increased fitness. Real speed or interval training play no part in this phase of development, however.

Gym work, circuits and strength training should be included in the basic stage. Most cyclists are all too familiar with this LSD stage and in fact some never leave it. Ideally, though, it should only last for 16-20 weeks (according to standards).

[2] *Intensity/Racing stage (12-16 weeks)*

Training needs to be stepped up a bit. Steady aerobic riding still makes up around 60 per cent of your development during this phase, which includes longer rides.

Most people have started racing by this stage and it is time to increase the training intensity by introducing specific speed and interval work. This will develop your body if it is increased, helping you to sustain high-intensity efforts for longer periods – essential in cycle racing.

> I (FW) often see a crop of injured riders around May or June each year. Although the names of the riders are different each season, the basic story is always the same ... He'd done all the right planning and his training was going well – too well, it seemed. He had built up his training mileage nicely, doing 15 to 20 hours a week, and then introduced intervals. In his first few races of the year he was already performing better and was enjoying local 'star' status, then wallop, first he got a cold which didn't seem to clear up, then he found himself struggling to keep up on training runs with people he was beating a few weeks before. His knee was playing up and he was ready to pack the season in ... A classic story of a rider bursting with enthusiasm and pushing himself harder and harder, paying no attention to his body's need for steady progression in training and its even greater need for rest and recovery. Your body is always telling you what it needs: **listen to it**.

Don't push the overload of high intensity training too hard too soon, or you will introduce a false peak. This will be short-lived, due to insufficient foundation, and can result in a form of psychological burn-out.

Practise riding skills during this stage: cornering, climbing, even eating and drinking while riding is a skill. Weaknesses should be worked upon, strengths should be perfected. Training should now be getting more specific to your chosen sphere of the sport. Discontinue gym work and circuit training.

Strength training, if continued, should be specific to the muscles and manner in which they are used in cycle racing. How long this phase lasts will depend on your racing standard and goals for the year, but could be 12 to 16 weeks. Towards the end of this stage steady aerobic riding should be reduced to 50 per cent.

3 *Intensity/Peak stage (6-8 weeks)*

Low intensity aerobic riding should be cut back to about 50 per cent of your training in this stage. Use it mainly to hold onto your aerobic development and to aid recovery from racing and high-intensity efforts.

The ability to hit peak form at the right moment − 'peaking' − is the ultimate in self-assessment: a combination of your own self-knowledge with the judgement of your coach, if you have one. In general, the foundations of your fitness decide how near you can get to your true potential. Your genetic background, your ability to train, your mental attitudes, your determination, all knit together to make you the kind of rider you eventually become. When you get to high levels of training, it is easy to do too much and overtrain, with all the attendant problems of illness, injury and staleness. So it is vital to heed your body signs and act upon them.

By now you should have your eye firmly fixed on the target race − the 'peak'. The idea is to achieve progressive improvements in your level of effort, interspersed with periods of lesser effort to help you recover and consolidate at the new level. Rest, relaxation and recovery are as vital a part of your training programme as time spent on the bike. You need intense speed work to 'sharpen the edge' and you can look at using short, non-target races to add speed and bite. Your efforts must be geared to the big race, but tempered by your level of experience in the sport.

You need to cut back on your training time once your speed, interval and race-pace effort are of increased intensity, and use low intensity aerobic riding for recovery. Racing, travel and diet all create their own stress levels during this phase, so allow yourself periods of mental and physical relaxation as well.

4 *4 Recovery stage (6-8 weeks)*

Your racing season is finished; time to relax and recover, but not to give away the gains that you have made. Forget the speed work and enjoy relaxed steady rides in company. You could start gym work, swimming, squash − in fact anything to introduce variety into your fitness routines. This is the time to reflect upon the past season and to plan for the next. A good time to fit in the dental check-up, physical assessment etc.

Training intensity

Two straightforward factors decide the physiological effect of training: how long you do it for, and how hard it is. So far so good? Right. A watch will tell you how long you're riding for; all we need is an equally reliable way of measuring how hard you are working. That's where most riders used to give up — unless they just happened to have fully-equipped testing laboratories round the corner. Because the fact is, it can be very easy to kid yourself you're flat out when in fact you are creeping along. Luckily, you don't have to go off and get a PhD in Sports Science to tailor your own training programme, as the whole system of understanding the physiological effects of training has been dramatically simplified.

Sports scientists discovered that intensity of training is related to lung capacity. In order to keep strict control and a true record of training intensity and lung capacity, training would need to be carried out in a fitness lab. Now research has shown that there is a reliable relationship — in cycle training — between oxygen consumption and heart rate. So, as long as you record your heart rate correctly, you have a simple and efficient method of monitoring training intensity levels. Many racing cyclists now have pulse meters, which make it much easier to monitor your pulse rate accurately. If you are not a proud owner of such a unit, it is simple enough to feel your pulse either at the wrist (in line with your thumb) or in your neck (to the side of your adam's apple). Using your fingers (not your thumb), feel for the pulse and once you have found it count the pulse beats for one minute, or, if you have just finished an effort, count for ten seconds and multiply by six.

Exercise physiologists have developed descriptions of intensity levels of training related to heart rate. Some have as many as eight levels, which would be almost impossible to monitor in a practical cycle sport situation. There is also the 'training language barrier' to overcome; one person's 'speed' is another's 'steady' which makes it very difficult to express the fine detail of a training programme with any accuracy!

Peter Keen, the sports scientist working with the British Cycling Federation's international squads, has created a system using only four levels of training intensity, which is easier for coaches and riders to monitor and acts as a 'training translator'. (His system is reproduced here with his permission.)

Four levels of training intensity

The four levels are described in terms of bike riding, but they apply equally to off-the-bike training. The training intensity at each of these levels is ideally controlled by working at the specified heart rate in beats per minute (BPM) relative to your individual maximum heart rate (MHR).

If you don't know your MHR, you can work on your theoretical maximum heart rate: either subtract your age from 220 or check against the chart (*see below*).

Check for age-related maximum heart rate

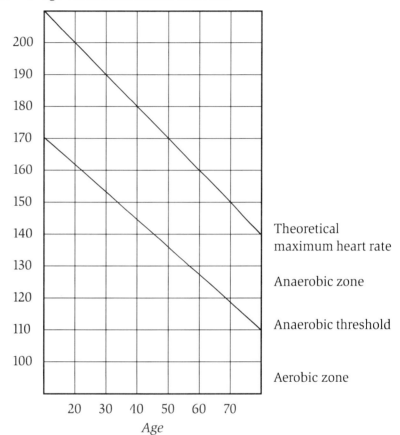

Heart rate in beats per min

Theoretical
maximum heart rate

Anaerobic zone

Anaerobic threshold

Aerobic zone

Age

Alternatively, for those who don't want to get that 'scientific', Peter Keen has given a description of how each of the four levels should 'feel' when being performed correctly. These sensations are consistent at each level during training, irrespective of the degree of fitness achieved.

When you are training at a particular level, you must keep within the indicated heart rate range. If the effort made is either harder or easier than the indicated heart rate for the intended level then the training effect will shift, so you will be actually training at a level either above or below the one intended.

<table>
<tr><td>

Training level 1

</td><td>

Heart rate − 40-50% MHR. Typically performed by riding at a heart rate of 50 to 60 BPM below your measured maximum heart rate. If your MHR is 200 then level 1 training effects would take place at below 150 BPM.

Sensation − relaxed enjoyable ride (preferably in company), breathing without discomfort. Can usually be carried out for several hours by experienced riders. Sensation of effort is very low and you should be unaware of your rate and depth of breathing, i.e. not stressful.

Limiting factors − if just started training, local muscular endurance and energy reserves. Another major factor is fluid intake. Carry appropriate food and drink on rides of one to two hours.

Frequency − used for basic fitness, recovery and relaxation. For beginners or riders with very low basic fitness there are some cardio-vascular benefits and plenty of this type of cycling is essential in the early stages of a programme if the destructive effects of overtraining are to be avoided. If used too often, would not contribute greatly to racing fitness.

Purpose − level 1 training is of little direct benefit to the well-trained cyclist, as it is below the intensity at which a significant strain is placed on the body functions that limit cycling performance. The real value is as an active recovery exercise, performed between more stressful workouts or at times when higher levels of training are undesirable for mental or physical reasons.

Furthermore, this low intensity level is ideal for learning basic skills, improving riding technique and acclimatising the body to long periods in the saddle.

Level 1 is the basis of most club runs and a very pleasant activity, but should not be confused with serious race training.

</td></tr>
<tr><td>

Training level 2

</td><td>

Heart rate − 50%-65% MHR. Level 2 is the training intensity at which the major biological mechanisms which determine your performance as a cyclist start to become taxed. For most riders this level equates to a heart beat in the range of 35 to 50 BPM below measured maximum heart rate.

Sensation − although fairly comfortable, breathing is slightly faster. Intensity is still relatively comfortable, but level 2 training requires a marked increase in concentration. Breathing rate becomes more rhythmic and is noticeably deeper.

</td></tr>
</table>

Limiting factors — usually energy reserves and fluid intake on the longer rides. Always take food and drink to avoid problems. Rides over two hours at this pace are possible, but there is a strong risk that the body's carbohydrate store will become exhausted. This causes blood sugar levels to become very low and leads to the distressing symptoms of muscle weakness and dizziness dreaded by cyclists as the 'bonk'. To avoid this situation, carbohydrate intake during and immediately following this form of training is essential and level 2 sessions should not exceed two hours when performed on a regular basis.

Frequency — level 2 is the cornerstone of endurance training and should be a regular part of all training programmes. At least three sessions per week are strongly recommended.

Purpose — training at level 2 results in a number of important physiological changes. These include:

* an improved oxygen supply to the working muscles by an increase in the heart's capacity to pump blood
* a rise in the total volume of blood
* the growth of small blood vessels within the muscles and the fine tuning of controlled blood flow in the body
* the ability of the muscles to use oxygen also improves through changes in the bio-chemical make-up in the muscle fibres.
* the use of fat as a fuel source in preference to the all-important carbohydrate store.

Training level 3

Heart rate — although expensive laboratory tests are required to exactly determine the correct intensity for level 3 training, a good approximation is to work as closely as possible to 25 BPM below your measured maximum heart rate.

Sensation — level 3 training is best performed as a continuous steady effort lasting between 20 and 30 minutes following a warm-up of at least 15 minutes. It feels as if you are cruising 'right on the edge'; a little faster and you would have to stop; a little slower and you would not be working hard enough. If you then feel that you could have comfortably gone on, you probably weren't riding hard enough. If during the session you become progressively exhausted, with heart rate, breathing rate and muscular pain rising continuously, then you're working too hard: ease off!

Limiting factors — the major factor limiting level 3 training is the discomfort associated with the body's failure to control the fatigue-causing processes – but that's what you're training to improve. Depletion of the body's carbohydrate store dramatically affects this type of training, so it is important to ensure you are fully recovered from any previous training session. If you perform level 3 training on indoor apparatus, as many riders do, heat build-up can be a problem. It is important to make sure you can dissipate the heat produced by the body and a large cooling fan is a very wise investment.

Frequency – although mentally taxing, level 3 training is widely believed to be the most effective way of increasing the power output at which you reach your critical work threshold. Take great care at this level as it is easy to go 'over the top'. Carefully build up level 3 training to determine how many sessions you can tolerate, but keep in mind the principle of a three-week build up, followed by reduced effort or time for recovery.

Purpose – the physiological reasons for level 3 training are somewhat complicated, but the basic principle is that every rider has a critical 'cruising' speed – a level of effort right on the edge between 'comfort' and 'too fast', beyond which you will blow up quite spectacularly. This phenomenon is well known to the middle-distance time triallist, who must become skilled at riding at a pace that does not exceed this critical work 'threshold'. The object of level 3 training is to exercise for a sustained period just at your critical threshold. Such a workout places a very high load on the body's ability to supply oxygen to muscles. Equally important, it stresses – and develops – the mechanisms which deal with muscle fatigue at high work rates.

Training at this intensity should dramatically improve your power and speed.

Training level 4

Heart rate – level 4 training is based on repetitions of intervals of hard effort interspersed with recovery periods, with the efforts up to your maximum heart rate.

Sensation – training at level 4 requires you to work at intervals of intensity above your critical threshold, so steady state exercise is no longer physically possible. Recovery between each work interval can be controlled using pulse rate. A good guide is to wait for your heart rate to return to 70 BPM below your measured maximum heart rate before you start the next effort. Depending on the discipline being trained for, the duration of the work efforts should be between 30 seconds and 3 minutes.

Limiting factors – level 4 interval training is the most demanding form of training both physically and psychologically, and must not be undertaken until you are 'fit' from basic training at levels 1, 2 and 3.

Juveniles should not use interval training methods without expert supervision and even then, caution must be exercised.

Frequency – in practical terms, think of level 4 training as the 'icing on the cake' of a training programme; it it tunes all the basic fitness work into real race conditioning. So add sessions to the training programme close to the start of actual racing. Begin with a 15-minute warm-up and follow actual training with a warm-down routine. Different types of interval training for different results are provided by Jim Hendry in the BCF Training Manual (available from the British Cycling Federation).

Purpose – as the primary objective of interval training is to repeatedly push yourself almost to the point of exhaustion, the major benefit is that you build a physiological and psychological resistance to short-term fatigue, a key factor in most race situations.

Two training effects

Through the various levels of training you will be able to monitor the different physiological effects. Two important training effects are a reduction in lactic acid production, and an increase in the rate of its removal from the bloodstream.

Lactic acid is a compound formed in the muscles when carbohydrate fuel is 'burned' anaerobically. It is one of the waste products that should be carried away by the blood. It can accumulate and cause stiffness after racing or training, particularly if you don't warm down. LSD recovery rides and massage help remove it from the body.

By hard training you raise your anaerobic threshold. Where once you could ride fast for 30 minutes, working comfortably and aerobically, before having to 'step over' and work anaerobically – and face the inevitable consequences of acid build-up and rapid fatigue – you will push the threshold back to 45 minutes, 60 minutes and so on. Generally speaking, if you train at levels 3 and 4 or work at between 70-85 per cent of your theoretical maximum effort, you will develop your anaerobic threshold and be able to ride faster for longer.

A four-week training cycle

Your true fitness levels will only improve if your training programme is progressive. That means you have to look at adding 5 to 10 per cent, either in volume or intensity. The problem with this is that if you get carried away you will eventually hit a point where your body would not be able to adapt to the increased training and injury or illness would result.

There is a way! To help avoid this situation, while still using the principle of progressive overload, experienced riders use a four-week training cycle that includes one week in four 'put by' to help the body to adapt. In a build-up routine the training is progressively increased for three weeks, then it is reduced for one week for recovery and adaptation.

At times this build-up routine might clash with your plans to peak for major races. If so, vary it by linking two routines together on a hard week/easy week cycle. Try different combinations during the training year to suit your own racing plans. Routines to include regular periods of adaptation are very effective.

Improving basic fitness

Racing cyclists need to spend most of their training time riding their bikes, because some of the 'training effects' required for cycle racing can only be obtained in that way. However, in common with most athletes, cyclists require a high level of 'basic fitness'.

For example, a sprinter cannot do sufficient quality work to bring himself to top form if his basic fitness is so low that he is unable to recover properly between training sprints. The middle-distance time triallist and the road racing man both need a high level of basic fitness to be able to endure repeated sessions of speed/endurance work in their training. The long distance cyclist is mainly concerned, in his training, with a high level of basic fitness coupled with the specific adaptations required for his particular event.

What then is this all-important 'basic fitness'? How and when should we work to improve it, and what methods can we use?

Basic fitness is the ability of the muscles to resist local fatigue, and the ability of the heart and lungs to provide energy materials and to remove waste products for extended periods of time. The ability of a muscle to resist local fatigue is directly related to its ability to generate power, which in turn is related to its strength.

Efficiency in the heart/lungs system is a complex subject with some unexplored aspects. Among the known aspects are:

1. the ability of the heart to pump a large volume of blood to the muscles
2. a good network of arteries and veins to supply blood to the muscles
3. a good network of arteries and veins supplying the heart muscle itself
4. the quantity and quality of the red blood cells
5. the quantity and quality of the tiny air-sacs inside the lungs

Basic fitness must be acquired first, before embarking upon the more specific training programme required for a particular kind of event. This means that basic fitness must be worked on for several months in advance, quite often, as in the case of most cycling events, during the winter months. As basic fitness is a prerequisite for many kinds of strenuous activity, various forms of exercise can be used to obtain it.

Amongst the methods available are weight training, circuit training and running. **Weight training** is a means of isolating muscle groups so as to provide them with a larger share of the work than they would normally get. Strength, power and endurance can all be improved by various combination of exercises, repetitions and sets of repetitions. **Circuit training** is a system for improving local muscular endurance and that of the heart/lungs system. This is done by arranging the exercises to provide work for different muscle groups in turn. Each muscle group is worked to near the point of local fatigue and then rested whilst another group is worked. Because the exercises are done non-stop − in a 'circuit' − this provides the heart and lungs with plenty to do, working all the time. **Running** is a means of putting a continuous 'overload' on the heart in a manner that is simple to organise, requires no apparatus and can be carried out at any time and in any conditions. The use of the large muscle groups of the legs and hips to lift the whole body weight ensures the kind of work by the heart/lungs system that would be difficult to arrange by almost any other method.

Whilst basic fitness can be much improved by each of these methods, the carry-over of this fitness into cycle-race fitness is not perfect. But the carry-over will be greater if you continue with plenty of riding whilst using these other methods.

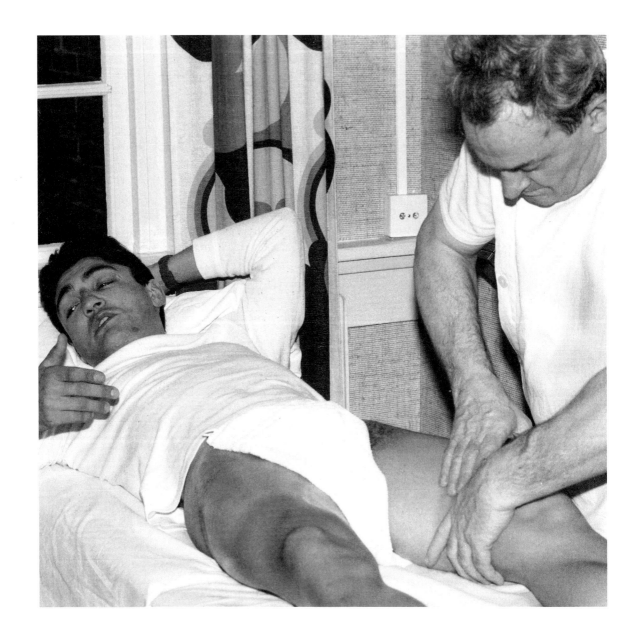

3   Massage

Sports therapists use massage to help cyclists relax, to help prevent injuries, promote quick recovery and also to help them get 'up' for competition. It's not just a case of rubbing legs, which is probably why it lost ground in favour of artificial methods such as drugs. Carried out properly, massage is a very effective form of therapy.

In this chapter, we'll be looking at the spectacular benefits that massage brings to the cyclist's body − and mind. We'll give an ideal massage routine that will help your recovery from training and aid performance. There are some massage techniques you can apply yourself, to your own muscles, if it's not possible for you to receive regular therapy, and we will show you how to do this.

Top international stage races such as the Tour de France are virtually marathons on wheels, except that unlike marathons stage races last for two or three weeks. Riders have to get to the line for the next day's racing and they must have cleared out their systems of the toxins produced by their efforts. Applied correctly, massage is the best way of achieving that.

Cycle sport has a long tradition of *soigneurs* − from a French word meaning 'to care for'. The institution of the soigneur is a very sensible idea. The team manager is left to manage and sort out tactics; the competitors get on with competing; the soigneur sorts out everything else: food and water, the right clothes, time to eat, suitable conditions to rest and relax, whatever else is necessary for the athletes to feel they are on top of the job.

The origins of massage

Massage is a systematic and scientific manipulation of the soft body tissues, performed mainly with the hands. Depending on the techniques that are used, it can soothe or stimulate the nervous and muscular systems and enhance your circulation. It is the earliest recorded form of physical therapy: the Chinese are known to have used it more than 3000 years ago. The Chinese used slow rhythmical massage techniques, as did the Indian masseurs. The purpose of such massage was to aid relaxation and it was probably closely connected with meditation and religion, as they believed treatment stimulated a spiritual energy flow. Egyptian and Persian medical texts also record the value of massage.

Massage has always been used by athletes, and since the days of the first Olympic Games the sporting Greeks and Romans regularly practised brisk stimulating movements.

We are now reaping the benefits of a combination of 3000 years of development with the precise evaluation techniques of Western science. We have a wealth of information on the physiological effects of different forms of massage. The modern system of sports and therapeutic massage uses deeper, more penetrating movements which, when applied correctly, require much shorter treatment times. Massage therapy has an important role to play in preventive and rehabilitation therapy.

The benefits of massage

Training and racing put your muscle tissue, tendons and ligaments under strain. This, together with the chemical changes occurring in the body during exercise, often leaves you stiff and sore.

If correctly applied, massage can greatly assist recovery by stimulating circulation, easing muscular spasm, and reducing stiffness and pain.

Superficial massage does little to ease the pain caused by strenuous exercise. The recovery process can only be speeded up by using deep soft-tissue manipulations. Researchers found that sports massage techniques performed on a muscle mass for ten minutes doubled the blood flow to the area for 40 minutes. This increased blood flow nourishes the tissue and clears waste products, reducing the stiffness which follows training.

Sports massage really comes into its own following prolonged periods of strenuous training; in fact the harder the session the greater the benefit will be. A warm-down and stretch routine can often ease the usual muscular stiffness following a light work-out, but won't on its own be enough to bring about a full recovery after a really hard session – especially if it is essential for the recovery to be rapid.

For many years massage was out in the wilderness, having fallen into disrepute due to untrained 'rubbers' creating more problems than they solved, and good sports masseurs are still hard to find. Many of the world's top sportsmen and women have regular massage during their stressful competition season. Olympic medallist Lasse Viren has a massage every other day from his personal masseur, Elmer Ukkola. He calls this 'preventive treatment', helping him to carry out an intensive conditioning programme uninterrupted by injury. East German athletes had regular massage as an integral part of their state system – a system that had an enviable record of delivering their athletes to major games in peak condition and keeping them injury-free for much longer periods than their European competitors.

Massage is important if you are following a tough systematic training programme. The sensitive, searching hands of the trained masseur will identify and treat the stressed muscles before real damage sets in. Firm, gentle manipulation separates the fibres to help flexibility, by relaxing the muscles shortened by the frequent, hard contractions of intense training.

Massage in itself does not increase muscle tone or strength, but by speeding up recovery from physical effort it does enable you to do more – to sustain a high level of training and competition with less risk of injury, which can in turn push up your strength and speed.

Later in this chapter we'll look at an ideal massage routine. You can use all the stroking, kneading, friction and finger pressure techniques on yourself if you don't have access to a therapist; the only difference is you'll find your back a little hard to do. First, though, let's look at exactly what effects massage and self-massage can have.

Massage and circulation

Medical research has shown that massage is one of the most effective ways to improve local circulation of the blood. Watching what happened through a microscope, researchers saw that even a light touch produced an instant dilation of capillaries – allowing more blood into and out of the area. The microscope showed that the effect lasted longer with a gentle increase in pressure and time. Without a microscope, you can often see the results of correctly applied massage techniques, because your skin will look flushed and 'full of blood'. Increased local circulation means that more nutrition and oxygen gets in, and more waste products are taken out, so your fatigued muscles are helped to recover and you will find you can overcome or avoid injury more easily.

This physiological effect is due in part to improved 'drainage' of blood and lymph from the muscles. This removes metabolites, the products of metabolism – in this case, the waste products of heavy exercise, such as lactic acid.

Lymph is a special type of fluid which circulates through a network of lymphatic vessels organised round lymph nodes. Lymph contains our specialist white cells, the ones familiar to us as vital parts of our immune system; they deal with toxins and micro-organisms. Experiments show that there is very little lymph flow when the muscles are at rest, but that it increases with massage. Unlike the blood circulation, which has the heart to drive it, there is no pump in the lymph system. Instead, the flow of lymph depends on gravity and on the squeezing caused by muscles in action.

Massage also increases pressure on another type of fluid known as *interstitial* fluid. This fills the spaces between tissues, just as interstitial – or connective – tissue provides the background 'net' or framework of support for our muscles and organs. Interstitial fluid and connective tissue are important, but often neglected, parts of our physiology. Toxins and acid waste products can build up in them; the pressure of massage encourages these to drain out and be absorbed through capillaries into the blood, and also to be absorbed by lymphatic vessels.

Most sports massage techniques, especially the more penetrating kneading movements, to some extent slightly traumatize the underlying tissue. At first sight, this is the last thing we want, but it is very slight and has some important benefits. This hard type of pressure encourages the release of H substance, a histamine-related chemical which is stored in most of our connective tissue cells and also in blood platelets and in our *basophil* cells.

The basophils are a special type of blood cell whose main function is to help defend against disease-causing micro-organisms such as bacteria. Basophils are the bike-rider's friends for another important reason: they help repair injured tissues, by removing debris and preparing the damaged site to be healed. How does the release of H substance help? It opens up the minute blood vessels of the skin and brings about a flushing of the whole area as tiny arteries open up due to the pressure activating a nerve reflex; it can even cause a slight swelling, showing that more tissue fluids – almost identical to lymph – are being released from capillaries.

All this happens when you use strong, linear stroking and frictions – small, intense circular movements made with the thumbs or fingers. Ordinary stroking or pressure techniques do not produce this reaction.

Oils and creams

There are probably as many massage oils, creams and mixtures as there are masseurs. The idea of using them is to avoid irritation to the skin and to enhance the contact between the hands and the area being treated.

There are umpteen lubricants made from olive oil, glycerine, coconut oil, almond oil, peanuts ... if it yields oil, it has probably been used at one time or another to massage. Other preparations include petroleum jelly, lanolin, and cold cream. Some people prefer dry preparations such as unperfumed talc, french chalk or baby powder.

The choice is personal, and therapists will tend to use their own favourite, the one that suits them and that they are used to, rather than anything that claims great healing qualities. The correct choice is the one which enables you to work with the greatest confidence, and one that your skin is not sensitive to. Care is needed in the selection of your massage medium so that you don't get a reaction, causing soreness or pimples.

One of the most popular and easily obtained lubricants for massage and self-massage is baby oil. This is designed for sensitive skin and is, therefore, highly unlikely to produce any adverse reaction, but again, be careful, for all baby oils are not made of the same basic oil and some can irritate certain sensitive skin.

The manufacturers often make ambitious claims for their warming embrocations or pain relieving creams. Although there is a place for them, it is not in a general massage situation, for unless they are used with care they can cause burning, the degree of which will depend on how sensitive your skin is. Rubifacient creams and some analgesic and 'soothing' preparations are usually counter-irritants, and work physiologically by bringing the blood to the surface of the skin and away from the muscles − the exact opposite of what we are trying to achieve with massage.

Some embrocations can also be used as massage lubricants. If it is a wet and windy day, it is probably worth using one of the milder massage creams such as Radian, Sports Rub or Musclor 1 to give just a gentle warmth. The warmer rubefacients such as Deep Heat, Cramer Red Hot, and Musclor 3 or Algipan may be applied to the tendon areas of the knees, but remember that they are not designed to be used for massage and the more you rub them in the hotter they will feel: they require only a light surface application and should not be used on hot days.

The light water based creams are fine for dry weather, provided that the strength matches the temperature: if it's a cool day use a cream producing mild heat, if a cold day a warmer product. For wet weather you need a petroleum-based embrocation, such as Cramer Atomic Balm, which will not wash off in the rain.

In cold weather, use warming embrocations around the knees, and on the calves and thighs. Also, if it's cold, wet and windy don't be afraid to use a medium embrocation on the lower back.

Most embrocations will come off when you have a shower after the race, some more easily than others. The creamier ones usually wash off with no problems, but the petroleum-based ones need to be removed with a cloth dipped in cologne or spirit. Sometimes even after removal they leave a very hot sensation, which can be countered by rubbing a cut lemon over the area − it sounds odd but it works.

Having decided on the preparation, don't use too much. Just use enough to lubricate, and to eliminate painful friction from the palm of the hand. Too much oil can make the hands so slippery that you can't make proper contact.

Look and feel: body awareness

Whether you are using self-massage or going for treatment, get into the habit of checking your body over, especially before a massage. You'll pick up a lot of useful information about your state of fitness and also stay alert to potential problems and be able to nip them in the bud.

Look at your skin for signs of contagious conditions such as impetigo, scabies, etc, infected or inflamed tissue areas. Look at the state of your skin – is it dry, oily, wet, hot, cold, hairy? Look for bruises and make sure you know what has caused them; some people have a tendency to spontaneous bruising and any strong pressure may make the problem worse.

Look for any possible circulatory problems. These can be indicated by pain in a localized area, swelling, excessive heat and may be causing you to feel ill. In this case you need medical attention and under no circumstances should massage treatment be given. Bad cases of varicose veins also mean no massage.

Look for swelling, muscle atrophy and colour changes, – in fact any irregularities of the skin – and make sure you have an explanation for them. Cold clammy skin may be an indication of a serious health problem.

You can tell a lot from the feel of your muscles. A cold area can indicate lack of circulation; an unusually warm area may mean infection, or a general inflammation or fever.

A routine sports massage combines examination and treatment, even if you are massaging yourself. You should start with a gentle superficial stroking, using the sensitivity of the fingers to detect the state of the tissues. You should concern yourself not only with the muscles but also the tendons, attachments, ligaments and connective tissue – the 'in-between bits'.

Small local ruptures of muscle fibres can be felt as swelling with increased local tension due to pain and at times inflammation. A large muscle rupture can often be felt as hard bulk of contracted muscle which may be over a much larger area of the muscle than the site of the trauma. At the actual point of the trauma there may be excessive swelling or a hollow area may be felt.

Any muscle rupture results in internal bleeding, which will appear as swelling of the muscle, or bruising on the surface which may spread over a larger area than the actual rupture.

The basic techniques

There are four basic movements in preventive massage:

1. Stroking movements − *effleurage*
2. kneading and pressure movement − *petrissage*
3. Frictions
4. Percussive and vibratory movements − *tapotement*.

Whatever technique you use, you must never lose sight of the main objective. This was summarised succinctly by Mennell (1880-1957): 'To use massage aright we must consider it entirely as a means to an end, that end being restoration of function'.

1 *Stroking*

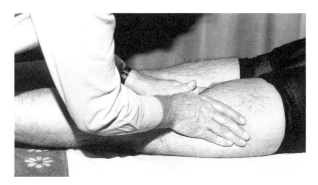

There are two types of stroking movement − light and deep stroking − each of which has its own physiological effects. Light stroking, which is the beginning and end movement of a therapeutic massage, increases the circulation of blood to the skin and affects the flow of lymph and venous blood. Deep stroking may be done with the whole of the hand as in light stroking, but with progressive pressure, or with the heel of the hand or pads of the thumb, according to the area undergoing treatment or depth of application required. Deep stroking massage can be painful. Don't overdo the pressure if you are due to compete on the day of the massage or the following day. Deep stroking increases the rate of flow in deeper veins and lymphatics, also increasing the mobility of the superficial soft tissues.

2 *Kneading*

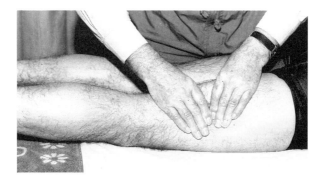

Kneading, or petrissage, is a more powerful movement of the muscle masses. The muscle being treated is grasped and lifted, rolled, squeezed or pressed in a systematic fashion, working along the muscle. Kneading disturbs cellular fluid, mobilizes muscle and intermuscular structures, increases circulation and waste removal.

3 *Frictions*

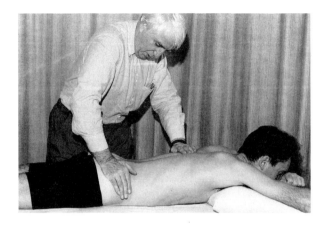

Frictions are generally small, localized movements most frequently circular and applied by the fingers, the heel of the hand, or the ball of the thumb. The technique involves firm local pressure, you move the skin over over the underlying tissues without friction at the skin itself. This treatment is effective where there is little muscle to get hold of − the joints, at the knee, ankle, elbow and wrist are good examples. It is also used along each side of the spinal column, under the shoulder blade and where spaces are too small to allow other forms of manipulation. Frictions are also effective in the large muscle mass of the buttocks following intensive racing or training.

Frictions loosen scar tissue, reduce local muscular spasm, and as you will see later, provide deep pressure over 'trigger' points to produce reflex effects. You mobilise and stretch using frictions.

Frictions this movement can also open up blood vessels, due to the release of a histamine-related substance from damaged cells.

4 *Percussion and vibration*

Percussion and vibration techniques (tapotement) include hacking, clapping, cupping, tapping and so on and can also include such variations as vibration and shaking. These techniques are not usually used in sports massage since the process generally brings blood to the surface: some people think they are in any case of cosmetic value only. They oppose the other techniques, which increase blood flow in the deep tissues − which is important for recovery from racing and training.

The rapid movements of vibration and shaking can be useful in sports massage because they assist relaxation. Some therapists use machines to produce the quivering effect in muscles, and small home units are widely on sale. The machines can be useful, especially on heavy muscle areas and when time is really short. Use them with caution, as little is known about the specific effect of different vibratory rates. Do not use them for a long period or if you are sensitive, or on the rib cage, chest, collar bone or spine; nor on the kidney area and prominent blood vessels.

Massage junkies

Don't get hung up on the idea that you have to have regular massage or you'll crack up.

In a stage race, massage is essential to help get your muscles back to normal in time for the next stage, but during most levels of training, massage is not all that important – it is only when the training effort has been so hard your muscles have remained tight that some corrective massage is needed if you are going to be able to ride the next day. In the main, however, stretching exercises will get most people back on the road quickly without incurring the expense of visits to a sports masseur.

There are advantages to regular massage, but there is the consequent danger of becoming dependent on it. If you are used to regular massage, and you go away to race where you are without your normal treatment, then you can become psychologically down because of the lack of it.

If you are going to a masseur, make sure that he or she is trained in the techniques of sports massage, and is recognised by one of the associations. There are a lot of enthusiastic, but untrained, 'rubbers' about who can easily rub the form *out* of your legs. Experienced sports masseurs can usually identify a rider who is used to going to a 'rubber', because he or she is usually insistent on a deep, hard technique. It isn't the fierceness of the rub that counts – although at times firm pressure needs to be applied – but whether the masseur's technique is easing the aches.

Before and after

Techniques of pre-race and post-race massage are radically different. Before a race you need a stimulating technique – brisk and of short duration. The muscles should be enlivened and not sedated. Bear this in mind even when you are putting on your own embrocations, since a similar technique is necessary.

Slow, purposeful movements are used after the race. If used before competition, they will have a relaxing effect, and you will need to ride yourself in during the opening miles instead of being ready when the flag drops.

Self-massage

Very few cyclists have access to regular massage, and even fewer have massage from a trained sports therapist. Luckily, most of the time massage is not essential, but during periods of intensive training, there can be times when you need massage if you are going to avoid injury, keep up your training level, and be able to recover. That's when self-massage comes into its own. No matter how skilled you become at it, you won't reach the same standard of treatment as a qualified sports masseur, but self-massage carried out on a regular basis can often be better than infrequent professional massage.

Through regular self-massage you can gradually develop a finer sense of touch, so that you can feel areas of muscular tension and the subtle changes in temperature that come about in your body when you're in hard training. You can perfect your technique to become fairly self-reliant, and you'll benefit from the 'conversation' you have with your body, which will help you pick up problems before they become serious. You cannot use the same techniques as a trained masseur: firstly because you will not have the knowledge, and secondly because you cannot put yourself in the same position to treat your muscles as can a masseur, who is free to approach from any angle.

The main areas that can benefit from massage are the legs, feet, buttocks, arms, back and neck. Apart from the back and neck, you can use self-massage effectively everywhere. The techniques you'll use need to be adaptations of the ones a professional masseur would use: light and deep stroking, kneading and friction.

If there is any secret to giving a good massage, it must be the development of sensitive fingers. Learn to ask questions with your fingers, feel the variations in the body tissues and contours of the limbs. Feel and visualise the muscles under the skin as you treat them. The more you practise this, the more skilled you will become.

Remember: pre-race, give yourself a short massage using brisk movements; after racing and training, for a relaxing recovery massage, take more time and use slow, rhythmical movements.

Self-massage for the legs

Start in a sitting position with your back supported and one leg resting on another chair. With your relaxed leg in a flexed position, stroke the full length of the calf muscle from the heel to the back of the knee. Always apply pressure towards the heart to help the blood flow return to the heart through the veins.

After about six light stroking movements increase the pressure, feeling at the same time for tight or tender areas.

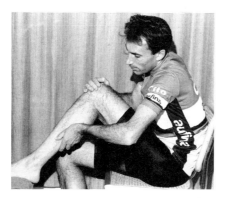 

After about six deep stroking movements, change to kneading. Grasp the calf muscle at the ankle area and give it a gentle, rolling squeeze. Continue up the whole of the calf and repeat three or four times.

If you have discovered any tight or tender areas which have not eased out, you can treat them with friction movements. Use the thumbs, fingers or heel of the hand in circular movements across the line of the muscle. Using firm pressure, work across the tight area three or four times, but take care not to make the area more tender.

After frictions or kneading, move back into stroking, going from firm to light strokes. Using the light stroking movement, transfer your hands to the thigh area. Repeat the procedure outlined for the calf muscles.

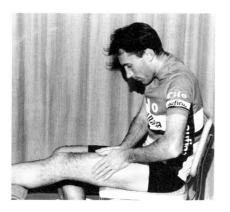 

Because the thigh muscles are a greater muscle mass and power source for cyclists, they may need a little more attention. Kneading can be supplemented with a pressure rolling technique over the whole of the thigh area.

Firmly grasp the thigh just above the knee with both hands. With firm pressure apply a rolling movement, at the same time moving the hands gradually up the thigh to the groin.

Having repeated this action three or four times, move into the stroking movement to the thigh, and finish your leg massage with a stroke to the full length of the leg, using both hands. Repeat on the other leg. After your leg massage do some gentle calf and thigh stretches.

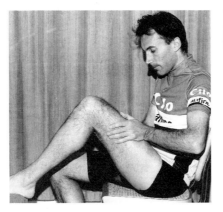 

Self-massage for the arms

Sit relaxed in a chair with your back supported.
Hold one arm across the body, and apply a stroking movement to the whole of the arm.

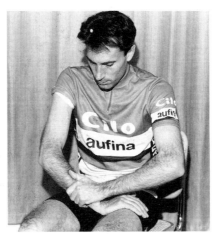 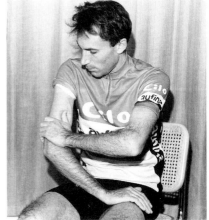

Use the same routine − stroking, kneading, friction (if necessary), ending with stroking − as outlined for the legs.
Repeat on the other arm. Afterwards, do gentle arm stretches.

Self-massage for buttocks and low back

In a standing position, start stroking movements from the buttocks to the low back, going from light to deep stroking. It is difficult at first to apply sufficient pressure for deep stroking, but with practice your technique will improve.

Follow the standard routine, adapting the techniques as necessary. The buttocks often need frictions, and the most efficient method is to use your fists.

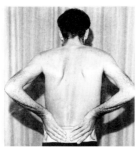 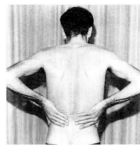 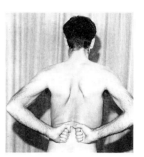

Follow up with some gentle stretches, particularly numbers 19 and 20 of the stretching routine (*see pages 63 – 64*).

Self-massage for neck and shoulders

This isn't easy, but there are times when you will be desperate for a massage to your neck, so persevere. Adapting the techniques of stroking, kneading and frictions will depend on the length of your arms and how

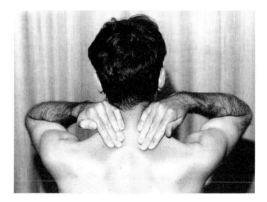

big your muscles are. The best method is probably to treat one side at a time, as you can then do the deep stroking and finger friction usually needed to ease the tension that can build up in the neck and shoulders during a long hard ride.

Stand or sit, whichever is the most comfortable for you. At the back of your neck, follow the flaring trapezius muscle from where it attaches to your shoulders right up to its insertion points behind the ears. Rubbing here always feels good and will help you relax.

As an optional extra, you can work over your feet and toes and round the ankle bones; you will probably be surprised at the painful spots you find. Don't dwell on them, but do hold or rub where it feels helpful.

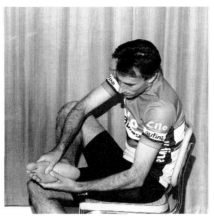 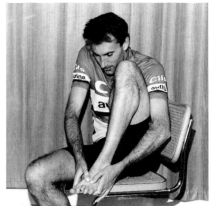

This routine will get you started. Follow the progression of the techniques from light stroking through deep stroking, kneading, frictions and light stroking again to complete your session. Experiment, as you get to know what works for your body, you may like to combine this routine with your post-exercise stretching programme.

Points to remember:

1 For massage to be effective, approach it in a quiet, relaxed manner.

2 Keep warm and comfortable.

3 Uncover only the part you are treating.

4 Surroundings should be pleasant, clean and quiet, to aid relaxation.

5 In order to avoid skin friction, use a lubricating agent such as talc (unperfumed) or oil.

6 Use only sufficient lubricant to ensure smooth movements. Too much will make the techniques difficult.

7 Begin and end treatment with light stroking.

8 Massage with pressure as you stroke towards the heart, taking the pressure off on the return stroke.

The routine
An example of a preventive massage routine is
1   light stroking
2   deep stroking
3   kneading
4   optional friction (if indicated)
5   deep stroking
6   light stroking

You can vary the intensity, tempo, rhythm and duration according to your needs. How long should it take? – a normal preventive or therapeutic massage should take no longer than 30 minutes in the hands of an experienced therapist.

If you are working on yourself, don't overdo things. Using modern massage techniques it is all too easy to over-treat, and often we get trapped into thinking that if ten minutes is good, twenty minutes is twice as good. This just isn't so. It is better to have two shorter sessions than one marathon session. Also bear in mind that some conditions take time to improve. Muscular tension, knots, scar tissue of long-standing, and soreness from a build-up of acid waste products, won't go away instantly, and treating an area for too long will create an adverse reaction, so be patient: learn to quit while you are ahead. Do a short treatment and rest easy in the knowledge that you have stimulated the body's natural healing ability – and that will go on working long after you've stopped using your hands.

When not to massage   In all forms of therapy it is always possible at times to do more harm than good. This is particularly so with massage: if the wrong type of condition is treated by this form of therapy, it can have serious consequences. Any stimulation of an infection may encourage it to spread, while treatment of a recent large bruise may stimulate aberrant bone formation.

Do not massage yourself or allow yourself to be massaged...

1 if your temperature is over 100 degrees F.

2 in the vicinity of skin infection (hot, red, swollen, tender, painful and possibly accompanied by loss of function).

3 near diseased blood vessels, e.g. varicose veins, phlebitis, thrombosis. (Usually cool, swollen, tender, painful particularly on stretching, and accompanied by swelling of the limb.)

4 in the vicinity of tumours (swellings either not painful or painful at rest).

5 in the vicinity of a specific disease.

6 if you react badly to the treatment.

7 where there is recently bruised muscle.

8 where symptoms make advice from a doctor advisable (for example, damage to the nervous system causing numbness and weakness).

9 if you have or suspect you have a head injury (for example, after a crash).

Medical advice should always be sought with such conditions.

Relaxation

Relaxation has got to mean more than slumping in front of your TV if you are going to make it as a bike-rider.

It may not feel like it, but watching the TV doesn't 'turn off' your brain and nervous system sufficiently for you to let go of your accumulated tension. But it will dull you and quieten you down enough to make you think you are relaxing.

Relaxation is an important part of your training programme and your first step is to re-learn how to do it. Then you are going to have to get used to the idea of scheduling in time and space to do it – just as you would a training run.

It may seem strange to have to learn to relax, but unfortunately most of us have lost the knowledge. After years of never completely relaxing, the body and mind have no memory of what a deeply relaxed state feels like, and you cannot now assume that you'll be able to relax when you want to. In fact your mind and muscles will still be in tension even when you are tired enough to sleep.

This continual state of body/mind tension interferes with your recovery from training and racing; it can set you up for illness and infections; stop effective digestion; and also stop you getting full refreshment from your sleep.

Relaxation researchers have found that by triggering the 'relaxation response', the body recovers more quickly – experienced meditators need less sleep, for example, since they reach such deeply relaxing states while still 'awake' – blood pressure normalises, sensations of pain ease off and the immune system benefits.

Ideally, you should set aside 30 minutes a day for active relaxation. You can use two 15-minute periods if that is more convenient. Pick a time when you are not going to be disturbed: no interruptions, no phone calls, no disturbing noises. Wear loose clothing, keep warm, and set an alarm if you need to, in case you fall asleep.

At the start of your relaxation training, it may help you to get expert help. Treat yourself to a relaxing massage from an experienced therapist or, if you are adventurous, to a session in a floatation tank or on a 'brain machine', where you can remind yourself what it feels like to be totally relaxed – then you know what you are aiming for in your daily sessions.

You need to find a method that works reliably for you; here are some suggestions.

1 Relaxation tapes. With or without music, they can give you a regular, timed session. Some will talk you through your body muscle by muscle, gradually talking you into letting go of accumulated tension. One of the

most effective we have used is called 'Catnapper' (from Mentronics), which includes a brain-wave synchronisation sound that quickly induces relaxation.

2 Yoga and/or meditation. Yoga postures promote suppleness and are designed to relax you physically and prepare you for meditation. Formal systems of meditation, such as TM (Transcendental Meditation), have proven beneficial effects on health.

3 Breath awareness and visualisation. An easy self-help technique which we'll explain here.

Lie comfortably, warm and well supported. Place one hand on your abdomen over your belly button. Breathe comfortably and naturally, and as you do so, feel your hand rising as you breathe in, and pressing gently into your abdomen as you breathe out. Let it happen. Allow your breath to 'settle' deeper in your belly, so that you are naturally breathing in a calmer, more relaxed way, from your diaphragm, rather than from that tense, uncomfortably high position in the chest. All you 'have' to do is, quite peacefully and gently, follow your breath as it flows in and out of you.

To add to the effects of relaxation, for the first few minutes of this exercise, consciously check out your body and relax any tight spots you find. Start with your head and work to your toes. Make sure you are not clenching your teeth – let your jaw hang loosely, spend some time seeing, in your mind's eye, the tight parts of your body such as shoulders, neck and thighs, 'expanding' and becoming 'heavier' and looser.

Notice the sensation you have in the parts you have 'worked' in this way: relaxation is as much in the mind as in the body, and if you 'see' part of your body relaxing, it will follow that image. You will find that as you lose yourself in your breathing, you relax into the present moment and your tensions and worries begin to melt away.

4   Stretching

Flexibility: you only notice it when you don't have it. And in the sporting cyclist it is often conspicuous by its absence.

Flexibility is the range of motion about a joint. It's whether you can move muscles and joints through their full ranges of motion, and it can be developed by stretching. You don't need to be an Olympic gymnast to ride a bike, but increasing your range of movement may help give you more power, and this will improve your performance.

Cyclists need specialist suppleness in certain areas of the body, especially the back and hips, to reduce the likelihood of the low back problems known as 'cyclist's back'.

During training, good flexibility cuts your risk of muscle strains and soreness, and increases circulation. If you are recovering from injury, flexibility exercises will also help to correct the muscle imbalances which may be associated with the actual injury.

Most of us know we should stretch more than we do, and compared with other athletes, cyclists are the world's worst. They just don't want to know, maybe because you can't do it on the bike. Very few even make a show of some kind of stretching before they begin their race or training run. At home or in the gym some riders may make a token effort with a couple of thigh stretches, but to be really effective you need to do at least 15 or 20 minutes of limbering up and stretching.

When working with teams from the USA, I (FW) was pleased to see the readiness of the riders to carry out a regular daily stretch programme. In contrast, few British riders stretched on a regular daily basis.

How flexible you are depends, like everything else, firstly on how nature has endowed you and secondly on how you have treated your body since you got it. You may even find that your own flexibility varies from side to side of your body, and as you test different muscles and joints.

Joint structure is one obvious cause of these differences: another is the amount of muscle and fatty tissue around the joint. It doesn't seem to matter what type of build you have. A flexibility programme cannot change the basic joint structure and won't alter your inbuilt potential, but it will help you reach the maximum suppleness that's right for you – not for anybody else, so don't be trapped into comparing yourself with anyone else.

A simple daily routine will work to loosen the muscles and connective tissue, such as tendons and ligaments, round the joints, improving your range of movement. However, it is important to know how to stretch to prevent injury due to overstretch. Stretching has to be directed to the particular needs of your body. Don't start forcing your joints beyond their normal range of movement, thinking you are doing yourself some good, as injuries can be caused just as easily through hypermobility (extreme flexibility) as through rigidity or restricted movement.

Because of the natural development of muscle bulk, men tend to find flexibility exercises more difficult than women. This does not mean that you cannot be both strong and flexible. It does mean that you need to develop both the strength and flexibility of the muscles and connective tissues. Muscles which are trained only for strength become shorter, this not only reduces their range of movement but in time makes them less efficient and more prone to injury. All strength-promoting exercise sessions must also include stretching of the same muscle group.

Older and stiffer?

As long as you have the correct stretch programme, you can develop your flexibility at any age.

Stretching is even more important as we get older, for there are chemical changes in the connective tissues of the body which help to reduce flexibility, among them a reaction known as cross-linking, the same type of process that turns soft latex into inflexible, hard rubber. With age, there is also an increased level of dehydration and an increase in adhesions.

Muscles are like bundles of long fibres. Adhesions are those sticky, maybe lumpy parts of a muscle, where the muscle fibres – which should be lying flat next to each other – bunch together rather than slide smoothly over each other when you move. These sticky patches can be caused by inflammation or – as is more likely – age, the accumulation of years of microscopic injuries, tears and bumps to the muscle tissue.

Stretching helps to combat these ageing processes. It stimulates the production or retention of lubricants between the connective tissue fibres to help prevent the formation of adhesions.

Relax and breathe

Before you begin your stretching routine relax. (*see* Relaxation *page 48*) It is not another form of competition. You are not trying to break your body with a supreme effort of will. You are going to work with your body, to encourage it to become gradually more supple. There is no rush and there should be no sense of strain.

Relax the muscles you are stretching. And don't forget to breathe normally throughout: correct breathing is essential for good stretching technique. Breathe out slowly as you are starting to feel the stretch or at the furthest point of the stretch: do not hold your breath.

How to stretch

Put yourself in a stable, well-balanced position. Move slowly and gently into your stretch position to 'feel' the point of mild tension. Ease back slightly and hold, breathing slowly and rhythmically.

You can hold the stretch from seconds to several minutes according to your experience and the condition of the muscle being stretched. As you hold in an 'easy' stretch, the muscles being stretched will gradually relax (if not you are creating too much tension), and when they do, gently stretch a little further, still only feeling mild tension.

If at this level the muscle or limb quivers or shakes, ease off the stretch. Static stretching does not hurt − unless you are doing it wrong. You are feeling for the point at which you can work without pain, but at which you are still gently extending your stretch.

Too little stretch will have no benefit, and too much will cause injury. The following points should always be remembered when doing your stretch routine.

1. Do not stretch cold. Stretch exercises should always be included in a gentle warm-up routine to avoid possible injury. A session of general mobility exercise and a few minutes, jogging would help warm the body enough to stretch. If the room is cold, or you are exercising in the open air, keep warm by wearing a track suit or other suitable clothing.
2. Slow static stretching, where you move to the point where you feel the stretch (not pain) and hold 30-60 seconds is probably the safest and most effective method of stretching.
3. Stretching should be performed both before and after a workout.
4. Use stable stretch positions to permit correct limb alignment.
5. Alternate muscle groups during exercises.
6. If you want to concentrate on a particular muscle group, go into a general stretch routine and come back to the target area several times during the routine with a progression of different exercises. Should one particular muscle be especially tight, stretch that group two or three times a day.

7. You will not get the full benefit from a flexibility programme if you wait until the season starts. Stretching should begin six weeks before the start of the season.

8. If you are injured, you should continue all flexibility exercises (except to injured areas if it causes pain) if possible, in order to maintain flexibility and prevent injuries when you return to competition.

9. Don't hurry. Concentrate on relaxing. Sometimes breathing out will help increase the amount of stretch.

10. Always start with gentle stretches, then gradually proceed to the more difficult ones.

11. Remember that stretching is not a competitive activity. Everyone will be at a different level and you should not attempt to stretch as far as anyone else. Also, stretch and flexibility is developed gradually, so you will have to stick at it to see results.

The stretches: a basic routine

1. Grasp hands, roll palms away from you. Extend your arms in front of you, stretching them out as far as you can, then extend them up and over your head as much as you can. Feel stretch in shoulders and side.

2   Grasp hands behind you, bring up and back as far as possible, keeping your back straight, and head facing forward, feeling the stretch in front of shoulders.

3   Grab the opposite elbow behind your head and pull across behind head. Repeat other arm. Feel stretch in shoulder and sides.

4. Slightly bend your knees to avoid stressing your low back, extend one arm above head and slowly lean to opposite side, stretching along side of body. Repeat, extending other arm.

5. Bring both knees to your chest, grab knees with hands, then lift head to knees, feeling stretch in low back.

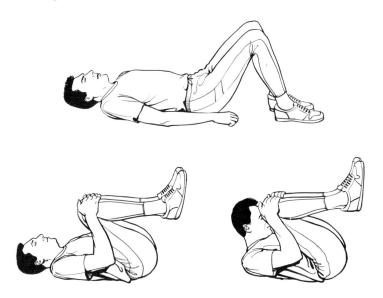

6 Lie on your stomach on the floor, place hands at shoulder height and slowly push upper body up and extend head back, feeling stretch in front of body.

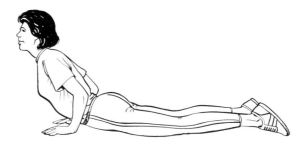

7 Sit in straddle with toes pointing straight up. **Keep back flat and head up** and reach for the foot to one side. Repeat to the other foot, and as you lean forward, feel stretch on inner thighs.

8   Lie on floor with arms out to side, bring one leg straight up, then slowly lower it across and toward the opposite arm. Stretch will be felt in low back and outside thigh. Keep shoulder and upper back on the floor.

9   Bend one knee and place the foot on the outside of the other leg. Then slowly rotate to the bent knee side, place elbow on the bent knee and push to help turn the body. Stretch will be felt in the low back and the hip of the bent knee.

10 Sit with one knee bent and foot on opposite inner thigh. Slowly lean forward and reach for the straight leg, feel stretch on bent inner thigh and low back and behind thigh on straight leg.

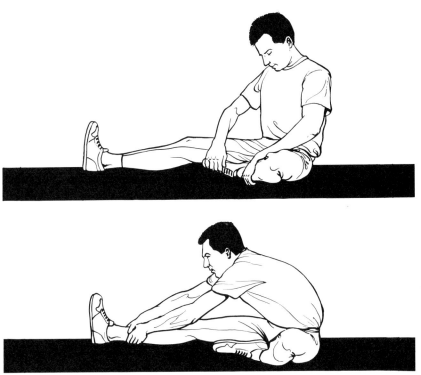

11 Place soles of feet together, grab the toes, and pull to inner thighs. Then slowly apply pressure to feel stretch on inner thighs.

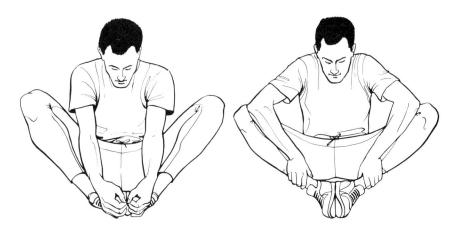

12 Lie on back, bring one knee to chest and grab under thigh, pulling to feel stretch in low back. Hold thigh in place and slowly straighten leg until you feel stretch in back of thigh.

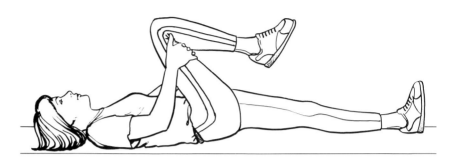

13   Stand upright with feet shoulder width apart, hands on hips, take a long step forward with the right leg at the same time flexing the knee to go down in a lunge position. Keep upper body straight, and lower hips towards floor. Feel stretch in front of hip and thigh. Repeat with other leg.

14   Stand sideways to wall or support. Slide the inside leg across the back of the outside leg and extend it away from the wall. Keep upper body straight, lean shoulders away from wall, and hips toward wall, feel stretch on inside hip and leg.

15 Stand, to face wall, or support, used for balance. Starting with the legs together, bend one knee by bringing foot up behind you and hold at the ankle. Keep upper body straight, and slowly pull the knee back, feeling stretch in front of thigh and hip.

16 Stand about two feet away from wall or support, and lean against it. Step forward with one leg. Keep heel down and feet pointed forward, and slowly bring hips down, bending front knee. Feel the stretch in the calf. Repeat with other leg.

17 Hands up, lean facing against wall or support, with feet about shoulder width apart. Keep heels down, bend knees, and slowly lean hips forward. Feel stretch in back of ankle. You may prefer to stretch one leg at a time, but make sure to stretch both legs.

18 Stand up straight, cross legs, slightly bend front knee, keep back leg straight, bend over to touch toes. Feel stretch in the back of the back leg. Change position and repeat with other leg.

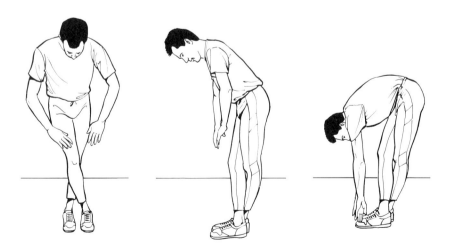

19 Lie on your back, either on the carpet or on the bed, with your knees bent. Make sure you are relaxed, with your head resting on a pillow, and bring one knee towards the chest holding at the knee, taking it as close to the chest as you can without discomfort (you should just feel the stretch, not pain). Hold for the required duration, release leg and lower to the bent knee position. Repeat using other leg.

20 Lie on your back, with your knees bent, body relaxed with head resting on a pillow. Place the ankle of one leg on the knee of the other leg, reach forward with both hands to the thigh of the supporting leg and gently bring it towards the chest as far as you can without pain. You should now feel the stretch in the buttock of the other leg. Hold for the required time, release leg and lower to the bent knee position. Repeat using other leg.

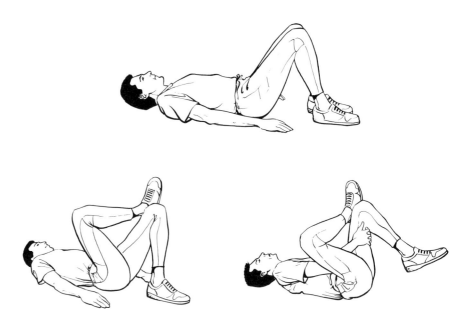

Myotactic reflexes: working with your muscles

Myotactic reflexes are a special part of the nervous system designed to help protect us from injuring our muscles.

Our reflexes act as coordinators of movement and are a form of automatic protection of the body. They come into play without conscious thought – they need no special instructions within our nervous system. This is not a 'design fault', but an important part of our survival system; unfortunately it can get in the way of the cyclist trying to improve flexibility. The good news is that the reflex system is easy to understand and so automatic that we can actually use it to get more stretch for our money.

If we always had to evaluate a situation when faced with possible danger our reaction could be so slow it would be too late. So we do not wait for the sensation of pain before we pull back our hands from a red-hot pan, and we don't think how we will fall in a crash – it is all done by reflex. There are several reflexes in operation all the time, assisting our body in its day-to-day tasks.

Within our muscles there are two particular myotactic reflexes which protect them from injury when they are doing strenuous training or being stretched: they are the *stretch reflex* and the *Golgi tendon organs*.

The stretch reflex is generated within the specialized muscle fibres called muscle spindles. Its main function is to help coordinate the movement of the muscle by giving constant feedback concerning the level of work being undertaken, and this feedback takes place during all muscle movements.

If you try to force a muscle to stretch too much or too fast for comfort, the muscle spindle relays information by an automatic reflex back to the spinal cord which immediately returns a signal to the muscle, telling it to contract in an effort to counteract the excessive stretch. If you try to ignore this protective reflex you will first feel pain; if you carry on, you will injure yourself.

The Golgi tendon organs are nerve receptors in the muscle tendons. They give virtually the opposite reaction to the muscle spindles. When you really exert your muscles and put too much pressure on the tendon, the Golgi tendon is triggered into action, creating the desired effect in the offending muscle. It does it it a roundabout way, by inhibiting the motor nerve stimulating the muscle, but the effect is the same: the muscle relaxes, eases out, in order to avoid injury to itself or its connective tissue. This simple system is one we can work with when we stretch.

When you reach the maximum point of a stretch (before you feel any pain!), and you maintain that stretch, the Golgi tendon organs will helpfully fire off their message to the resisting muscle to stop contracting. The resisting muscles – the ones you are trying to stretch – will then relax and ease out. You can actually feel this happening: as the tension dissipates, you relax, stretch, and the muscle can then be lengthened a little more.

Knowing about this reflex, it is easy to see that a few seconds spent on a long, slow stretch will bring you a real result. It is much more effective than the quick, can't-be bothered, token stretch so many bike-riders go in for.

This stretch has to be coordinated with the stretch reflex of the muscle spindles. You need to take it slowly and not push yourself too far, otherwise you will stimulate them and the muscle will be pulled back. The action of these myotactic reflexes is a very delicate balancing act.

The art of PNF-ing

PNF stands for Proprioceptive Neuromuscular Facilitation. Some exercise researchers claim that PNF techniques are *the* most successful for developing flexibility.

PNF fans also claim that it enhances active flexibility and helps to establish a pattern for coordinated motion, along with the triggering of several important neurophysiological mechanisms.

All this may well be the case, but unfortunately PNF techniques also have some disadvantages. The principle ones are the greater risk of injury, and the need for a knowledgeable and well-trained person (not easy to come by) to assist you. But if you can work with an intelligent, non-competitive partner, these techniques are worth using – carefully.

We must warn, though, that several exercise specialists believe that PNF stretching leaves the muscle open to injury and recommend that it should not be attempted without trained assistance.

PNF was originally developed as a physical therapy technique to help with rehabilitation after injuries, and over the years several different PNF procedures have been introduced for use in sports medicine. Two of the most widely used are the contract-relax technique and the contract-relax-contract technique, which have been found to be the most beneficial in improving the range of motion.

Static versus bouncing stretches

Highly-trained dancers and gymnasts can get away with bouncing stretches. For the rest of us, the rule is … **don't** bounce. The bouncing, or ballistic, stretch involves building up momentum through a swinging or bouncing movement which uses the weight of your body to increase the force of the stretch. Ballistic stretching creates a high, fast force, putting more than double the normal tension on the muscle. The bounce evokes a strong stretch reflex contraction, pulling the muscle back and shortening it so there is no time for a protective response to be activated by the Golgi tendon organs.

Research in recent years has proved that slow, 'static' stretches are the best and safest. The safest way to stretch is to gradually develop resistance to the full point of the stretch (not pain) and hold it there for five to ten seconds before releasing it.

By using static stretching you minimize the reaction of the stretch reflex, and the length of time you spend in the stretch is enough to allow the Golgi tendon organs to relax the muscle a bit more for a greater stretch. Static stretching reduces the possibility of 'overstretch' injuries. It helps to relieve muscular soreness and also takes less energy, which can be important when you are warming up for a race or trying to recover after hard training or competition.

5 Diet and supplements

Whenever riders get together with coaches, conversation invariably swings to diet supplements, vitamins and tonics. And providing cyclists are not looking for the 'secret' to transform them into Greg LeMond, discussion of diet is worthwhile, since the standard of our food intake is relevant to our standard of performance.

There is no magic food that will enhance performance. Top cyclists often have completely different dietary regimes, varying from steak with everything to semi-vegetarian, and if you were to check on what the leading riders in the Tour de France were in the habit of eating during training and racing you would be amazed at the variation.

Top riders are good at what they do mainly because of their genetic ability, mental attitude, and ability to train and race to their limit, not because of what they eat. That said, your diet can stop you achieving your full potential as a sporting cyclist if you do not give your body what it needs to do its job.

Your body will make three main demands on your food intake:
1. Energy: from carbohydrates, fats and proteins.
2. Growth and repair: by means of proteins, trace elements and water.
3. Regulating the body processes: by means of vitamins, trace elements, water, and certain proteins.

Be sure that your meals are of good quality, fresh and freshly prepared foods, containing their full complement of vitamins and minerals. Cooking is itself a form of processing; you can help yourself by making sure your food is cooked as little as necessary to make it digestible and safe from disease-causing micro-organisms. For instance, fruit and salad vegetables can be eaten raw, other vegetables can be lightly steamed rather than boiled.

Eat a wide variety of foods. Don't get stuck in a rut of eating the same foods day in, day out, or you increase your risk of running into nutrient imbalances. Remember there is no single food that will supply all the needs of the body. A good quality multi-vitamin and mineral supplement taken daily is recommended to ensure that your minimum nutrient needs are covered.

> *What chewing can do for you*
>
> One simple way to greatly increase the amount of nutrients that you absorb is to chew well the food that you eat. The digestive process starts as soon as you start to eat. So chewing your food well helps this process and enables you to get full benefit from the nutrient content of the food.
>
> So many people eat in a hurry, chew a few times and swallow the food. Eating this way not only robs us of the full taste of the food, but also important nutrients. If we were to increase the amount of chewing by 50% or so, we would not only get greater satisfaction from our food, but considerably increase its contribution to our sporting efforts.

Check your diet to make sure you have regular square meals. See that your energy and mineral salt requirements are fulfilled before, during and after racing.

Your body prefers it if your meal times are fairly regular, so get into a reasonable routine of breakfast, lunch, dinner and if necessary a very light supper (try to avoid eating late at night, or when you are very tired, especially high protein meals, which take a comparatively long time and a lot of energy to digest).

Some riders go into the mystique of taking various vitamin preparations and tonics with the idea that these will improve their general performance, but providing the preparations are purely nutritional and are not chemical stimulants, they won't improve performance.

However, there is evidence that some nutrients and herbal preparations – such as the mis-named Siberian 'ginseng', for instance – can help serious athletes adapt to the strain of competition and training. Be careful, some products on the market which contain ginseng are on the Banned List (*see page 138*).

From the scientific research it seems that some individuals, when stressed by hard physical activity, may benefit from larger than average intakes of specific nutrients. Nutritional supplements may also ensure that a deficiency, or sub-clinical deficiency, does not occur and may help you maintain your level of performance without running into illness or injury.

Again, though, we emphasise that this sort of nutritional and herbal 'tuning' is a highly individual matter. It is the icing on the cake, not the main meal. It is worthwhile pursuing your own research into this field, preferably with the guidance of a sympathetic coach or health practitioner, but remember, there is no substance yet discovered that will turn an also-ran into a world-beater.

Choosing your food

We all have our likes and dislikes but as far as our body processes are concerned, mouth-watering dishes are just chemical compounds. And as with all chemistry, if the right amount of chemicals are not put into the formula then the end results are not satisfactory. This is the case with the human body. If protein is not taken in, then the repair of tissue and general wear and tear will not take place, and without carbohydrates and fats you won't get the energy you need.

With a few important exceptions, the general diet of a sporting cyclist doesn't need to be that different from an above average 'normal' diet: that is to say that the 'square meal' that most people are accustomed to eating can be the nutritional standard that is required for athletic pursuit, as long as it is stoked up with higher levels of carbohydrates.

In the past decade the average western diet has undergone many changes which are not altogether for the good, and what used to be regarded as a normal balanced diet no longer exists. Instead, the average diet now lacks fresh vegetables and fibre; it is chockful of processed foods that may lack essential nutrients; it is likely to be too high in fat, sugar and salt; it contains potentially harmful residues of pesticides, insecticides, food-chain antibiotics, and it probably contains 'non-foods' such as preservatives, colourings, flavourings and fillers.

The sporting cyclist should look at reducing his or her intake of refined fats (in cooked and processed foods) and increasing the proportion of quality, 'whole' carbohydrates containing essential nutrients – wholemeal bread, flour and pasta rather than refined 'white' versions, for example. This nutritional shift becomes more important when training at high intensity or riding at race pace: the longer the duration and the greater the intensity of the training session, the greater the need for energy foods.

Preferring 'wholefoods' to refined food products won't turn you into a health food crank; it's common sense. To take just one example, one of your main energy sources as a cyclist should be the complex carbohydrates found in wholemeal (not just 'brown') bread and pasta. Your body takes these foods and breaks them down into smaller components, extracting the nutrients it needs according to its own scale of priorities.

In order to break down complex carbohydrates, your body's chemical factory needs nutrients such as the whole complex of B vitamins and the mineral zinc. Where are these to be found? – in whole grains. From what foods have they been taken out? You guessed it – 'refined' white bread, white rice and white flour. Some of these claim to have been 'enriched', another way of saying that a small proportion of what's been taken out has been put back in.

If you are a keen racing cyclist you must start to be selective about what you eat. There are many highly processed products available which contain few or no nutrients – they are virtually 'non-foods'. Unfortunately, they are usually attractively packaged and may be more convenient. What you are looking for are nutrient-rich foods; calories alone are not enough – you must also supply the enzymes, vitamins, minerals and co-factors necessary for you to metabolise your food and rebuild yourself. We all hear stories of the champions who train on junk food. What we don't hear about is what happens to them after their short, dynamic careers are over. Put under great stress, such as a hard racing and training programme, the human body can become very efficient at extracting what it needs to keep going from even the poorest quality fuel. However, giving yourself lashings of calories without vital

---

FOODLIST

We have put together this foodlist as a guide to what certain foods will do for you. In the 'allowed' list are foods recommended for their higher nutrient or fibre content, and their suitability for most sports people. The 'avoid' list consists of foods with either toxic or low nutrient content, which could present digestive difficulties when racing or training.

BEVERAGES

Allowed – weak tea, herb tea especially chamomile or mint, fruit and vegetable juices, non-fat milk, yoghurt or buttermilk.
Avoid – alcohol, cocoa, coffee, full fat milk, fizzy soft drinks, juices with artificial colouring and sweeteners.

FOOD

Grains

Allowed – wholemeal, bran or rye bread, cereals: oatmeal, branflakes, sesame, pumpkin, sunflower seeds, brown rice, muesli.
Avoid – white bread and white flour products.

Dairy Products

Allowed – most hard cheese in limited amounts, cottage cheese, unsalted butter, poached or boiled eggs (not more than one a day).
Avoid – blue vein and soft cheeses.

Oils

Allowed – cold pressed olive oil (preferably extra virgin), cold pressed, unrefined safflower or corn oil spreads.
Avoid – lard, refined and saturated fats and oils, hydrogenated margarine.

Nuts

Allowed – all fresh and raw nuts, except peanuts.
Avoid – peanuts, all salted and roasted nuts of any kind.

nutrients is like filling your car to overflowing with petrol but failing to top up the oil and water, missing out brake fluid and economising on air in your tyres.

Many dietary fads followed by top riders are happy accidents: through trial and error they have hit on a way of eating that suits them. That does not mean that it will be right — or 'balanced' — for you. We set out the basic principles that are likely to work for most people, but we also encourage you to experiment.

Food for energy

If your body is not receiving sufficient food as fuel you will not be able to race or train effectively. So your energy input must be balanced with your output. Not all foods are equally useful as primary fuel so — **be selective**.

Fish
Allowed — all white fish, salmon, herrings and tuna (grilled, baked or steamed).

Fruits
Allowed — all fresh or re-hydrated dried fruit, and unsweetened frozen fruit.

Meat
Allowed — chicken and turkey. Lamb, beef and veal in limited quantity.
Avoid — pork, processed meat, sausages and mince. The reason to avoid processed meats is because of the various additives that they contain. These substances can inhibit the body's enzyme activity and cause health problems.

Vegetables
Allowed — highly recommended, all raw or cooked fresh or frozen vegetables.
Avoid — all canned vegetables, potato crisps and chips.

Seasoning
Allowed — herbs, garlic, onion, chives, parsley.
Avoid — pepper, paprika, salt, all sauces made with vinegar.

Soup
Allowed — all unspiced soups.

Sweets
Allowed — unpasteurised honey, maple syrup, jam and marmalade.
Avoid — refined sugar, chocolate, jelly, ice cream.

General note
Avoid — Smoking and areas containing smoke. Excessive car and aircraft exhaust. Foods sprayed with pesticides. Additives in foods. Foods with chemical preservatives.

It used to be the case that the self-respecting bike-rider tried to cram down steak and salad at every opportunity (especially if someone else was paying, of course). That was before research into the nutritional needs of sports people became respectable. Almost everybody believed that if you took part in sport you needed vast amounts of protein. We now know that this is not true and that what we need most are energy foods: that means carbohydrates or fats.

Both these types of food supply energy, but research tells us that for making strenuous physical efforts carbohydrates are the most efficient; in any case, as mentioned earlier, too high an intake of animal fats is bad for you. It's best that during the 48 hours before competition your meals are high in complex carbohydrates – potatoes and other root vegetables, wholegrain cereals and pasta, etc. This carbohydrate will be converted into glycogen and stored in the liver ready to be drawn on during competition. This store can then be used in a short-distance race, with a possible topping up of glucose.

The disadvantage of taking glucose in tablet or powder form is that it requires a lot of liquid, which can upset the system, so it is more efficient to use a glucose drink. Body stress can cause loss of energy, which may be created by many things including a high sugar intake, regular use of common stimulants such as coffee, strong tea, alcohol, chocolate, cigarettes, drugs and so on. Avoid them where possible, as they won't help your performance or your recovery. The stress caused by stimulants can, in time, upset the glands leading to possible hormonal problems.

Supplements

We each need certain amounts of vitamins and minerals to satisfy the requirement of our body.

The Recommended Daily Intake (RDI) for nutrients has been widely accepted as being the average basic requirement for a healthy person. In fact, RDIs are simply the absolute minimum amounts of certain nutrients necessary to stave off obvious deficiency diseases. They are not the amounts necessary for the best possible state of health, let alone for maximum performance. RDIs differ widely from country to country and seem to be being continually revised – upwards.

We are all individuals and our needs can vary greatly; as a result, some people will stay healthy on diets that meet the RDIs, while others will become ill but will not have their problems traced back to their diets. This can be especially true for sports people. A rider could be competing in a sub-clinically deficient state – that is without displaying obvious deficiency symptoms.

Modern farming and food processing techniques are not designed to safeguard the nutrient content of foods. We assume our food contains the optimal amounts of nutrients, but the growers produce new strains of tomatoes for supermarkets, for instance, to look good and keep their shape and colour during harvest, storage and display − not for their nutritional content. So when you take into account the demands made on your body by racing and training, plus the extra nutrient drains of pollution and stress, there is a strong case to be made for a rational 'insurance' policy of dietary supplementation. This is particularly advisable for cyclists who travel widely and have little control over the quality of the food they eat; they may also by virtue of fatigue or distaste for local food eat less than they need.

Mega-doses of supplements are not a substitute for a proper diet, but sensible supplementation can back up your efforts with food. Vitamins and minerals are not sources of energy; they work mainly as metabolic regulators, with an important role in energy transformation. They act as co-enzymes in enzyme systems and usually only small amounts are required by the body. They are essential for good health and fitness.

Several vitamins can now be made synthetically. Current research indicates that whilst the body is unable to distinguish between 'natural' and synthetic forms, there is evidence that 'natural' forms of these chemical compounds behave differently in the body and may confer some benefits. Dr Len Mervyn, PhD, a clinical biochemist involved in original research into vitamins, gives as an example the natural form of vitamin E (d-alpha tocopherol), which is known to be biologically more active and to be retained longer by the body than synthetic vitamin E. Other nutrients benefit from co-factors present in natural formulations, which help them to be absorbed and used: vitamin E, for instance, is absorbed better when presented, as in nature, in fats or oils such as wheatgerm oil. So when choosing your supplements, look for those that are biologically 'available' to the body: as with nutrients in foods, it's not how much you consume that's important, but how much you are able to digest, and use.

When it comes to supplements, the cheapest does not always represent the best value. Look for supplements that contain the natural co-factors necessary for your body to be able to absorb the nutrients; this may mean choosing supplements that are 'packaged' in natural foods and/or herbs, which will help them be absorbed, and those that are supplied with the other nutrients needed to balance them. Supplements of selenium, for example, may increase your requirement for zinc, so the best types contain both, plus other necessary nutrients such as vitamin C. Again, check with manufacturers' or relevant literature for details of what you are paying for; you may find that one supplement is more expensive than the others, but that it is the only one that has scientific studies confirming its bio-availability. L-seleno methionine, for instance, is the type of selenium best absorbed by the body.

Absorption can also be blocked by non-nutrient factors in your diet (such as medical drugs, caffeine in tea and coffee, alcohol and so on) and in the supplements themselves. This is another reason why the cheapest supplements are not always the best, since they are likely to contain not only the cheapest possible forms of nutrients, but will also have compromised on the additives such as preservatives, fillers, sweeteners, coatings, binders and so on used to hold the tablet or capsule together and make it palatable. If you are taking a number of tablets or capsules every day, these factors can start to make a difference. Manufacturers are now making efforts to provide 'pure' supplements, and many have also incurred extra production costs by avoiding the use of those ingredients – such as gluten, a protein constituent of wheat, corn and eggs, to which many people are sensitive or outright allergic.

Some riders take quite a wide selection of individual supplements without being aware of their potential effect (or lack of it), but the very fact of taking them has a psychological boost, which in turn can help performance. But let us stress that this is psychological, not physiological, and it can get very expensive. Using supplements sensibly means you need to research the area, or find a coach who can help you.

There are times when the taking of extra vitamins is desirable, possibly during a period of staleness when a B-complex tablet supplying at least 50mg (milligrams) of the major B vitamins with 50mcg (micrograms) of hydroxy B12, and a tablet of 250mg of vitamin C could be an aid.

Another good case for supplements is during stage races when your digestive system can come under strain and cannot absorb the required nutrients, or during periods of hard racing when your red blood cell count can drop. If you are using oral contraceptives, you should know that they have been associated with deficiencies of many nutrients, especially vitamin C, B6, B12, folic acid, riboflavin and the mineral zinc.

Vitamin injections should be avoided if possible, and administered only by a doctor, as there is not only a risk of the needle severing or impinging on a nerve, but also that the substance being injected is not compatible with you.

Iron

It is not always possible to work out exactly what nutrients we need, as our requirements vary from day to day. Sometimes we feel tired, suffer a loss of form and, to make matters worse, we are unable to sleep. This can be from over-training, or it can be iron deficiency (anaemia). There have been some controversial research reports that certain types of training may cause iron loss through gut bleeding or internal red blood cell destruction. The phenomenon of red blood cell breakdown and haemoglobin loss in urine due to constant pressure on the saddle over long distances has given rise to the term 'bicycle seat haematuria'. This condition may affect the excessive mile-eater so if this describes you be on your guard against iron deficiency.

Iron deficiency amongst teenagers can be due to a bad diet and the demands of a rapid growth rate. On top of that strenuous training can create a temporary drop in plasma and haemoglobin and result in the so-called 'sports anaemia'.

If you are in these possible risk groups, make sure that you have plenty of iron-rich foods in your daily food intake. Ask your doctor for a blood test to determine the actual cause, as the taking of iron supplements without medical guidance is not recommended. Iron supplements vary widely in their ease of absorption.

Iron and menstruation   Women riders sometimes become anaemic because of menstrual loss. The monthly period affects different women in different ways, and it is important for every woman cyclist to be aware of exactly how it affects her personally, both physically and mentally. No one has ever shown that it is injurious to compete strenuously during menstruation, so do not assume that an important event will be 'ruined' if it clashes with a period. Some women find their performance deteriorates during their period; others actually perform better. The cause can be mental or physical. You need to monitor just how menstruation affects you personally, and act accordingly. If you suffer during your periods and you are selected for international races, then you should discuss this matter with your cycling federation's doctor, who can advise you on the possible alternatives. There are ways of deferring the menstrual period until after a major event, but this is a matter for planning and medical supervision.

Strenuous exercise can affect the regularity of periods. Light training doesn't usually affect them, but exceptionally heavy training can advance periods, upset their regularity, and sometimes cause them to cease altogether. Any such irregularity usually corrects itself when training is reduced again. There is no proven adverse effect of such irregularities although it is possible that there is a connection between amenorrhoea (cessation of periods) and osteoporosis (brittle bones) but they are worth mentioning to the federation doctor or your own GP just in case your racing is not the culprit.

One definite benefit of training and racing is the reduction of pre-menstrual tension. Whether this is because training affects levels of hormone production, or whether the exercise helps generally, is not known. If pre-menstrual syndrome remains a problem for you, then it is worth investigating the use of supplements such as vitamin B6, GLA/evening primrose oil and magnesium.

Vitamins

Vitamins are vital to the regulation of the body processes, and their deficiency can have startling results. When watching your intake of vitamins, bear in mind that they are lost in cooking or storage; so try to eat food fresh and, wherever possible and palatable, raw. It is also a healthy move to go where possible for whole foods − i.e. those without additives. In this way you should be sure of a regular vitamin and mineral supply.

Here is a list of vitamins in detail, together with their functions, sources and (most important) some of the substances which reduce their effect:

Vitamin A (Carotene) − fat-soluble
Promotes: skin health, resistance to infection, bone development maintains good eyesight
Sources: melon, peach, carrot, lettuce, broccoli, parsley, fish-liver oils, butter, margarine, offal, certain nuts
Depleting factors: cortisone and other drugs, excess alcohol, iron consumption, coffee, tobacco

Vitamin B1 (Thiamine) − water soluble
Promotes: carbohydrate metabolism, energy production, growth, appetite, digestion, nerve activity, gastro-intestinal tonus
Sources: wheatgerm, soya beans, flour, brewer's yeast, beans, potatoes, cereals, nuts, some fish
Depleting factors: alcohol, antibiotics, birth-control pills, coffee, stress, diarrhoea
NB increase intake when increasing intake of carbohydrate

Vitamin B2 (Riboflavin) − water soluble
Helps: maintain skin, digestive tract and vision, co-enzyme in respiratory enzyme system
Sources: offal, avocado, soya beans, nuts, cheese, milk, potatoes, cereal
Depleting factors: alcohol, birth-control pills, tobacco, coffee

Vitamin B3 (Niacin) − water soluble
Helps: circulatory system, growth, maintenance of nervous system, co-enzyme in tissue respiration and fat synthesis
Sources: meat, fish, peanuts, brewer's yeast
Depleting factors: alcohol, antibiotics, birth-control pills, coffee, corn, tissue trauma

Vitamin B5 (Pantothenic acid) − water soluble
Promotes: antibody formation, carbohydrate metabolism stimulation of adrenals, keeps skin and nerves healthy

Sources: liver, spinach, broccoli, eggs, milk
Depleting factors: alcohol, coffee, sleeping pills, stress

Vitamin B6 (Pyridoxine) – water soluble
Helps: co-enzyme in protein, fat and carbohydrate metabolism,
controls magnesium levels
Sources: liver, herring, potatoes, pork, whole-grain cereals, eggs, milk
Depleting factors: ageing, alcohol, sleeping pills, radiation exposure,
birth-control pills

Vitamin B12 (Cyanocobalamin) – water soluble
Helps: co-enzyme in protein synthesis, blood cell formation,
maintenance of nerve tissue
Sources: offal, egg yolk, cheese, milk, fish, meat
Depleting factors: ageing, alcohol, coffee, laxatives, sleeping pills

Vitamin C (Ascorbic acid) – water soluble
Helps: absorption of iron, calcium diffusion, synthesis of collagen,
maintenance of blood vessels
Sources: citrus fruits, blackcurrants, rose-hips, cabbage, brussels
sprouts, tomatoes, potatoes
Depleting factors: antibiotics, anxiety, aspirin, burns, cortisone, sulfa
drugs, tobacco, stress

Vitamin D (Calciferol) – fat-soluble
Promotes: normal growth through bone growth, absorption of calcium
and phosphorus, gland and nerve function
Sources: tuna, halibut- and cod-liver oils, herring, sardines, butter,
margarine, milk, eggs, sunlight
Depleting factors: mineral oils

Vitamin E (Tocopherol) – fat-soluble
Helps: normal growth maintenance, normal muscle metabolism,
maintains integrity of central nervous system and circulation,
maintains kidney tubules, lungs, genital structures and liver
Sources: lettuce, corn, green peppers, peanuts, wheatgerm
Depleting factors: air pollution, birth-control pills, iron

Vitamin K (Menadione) – fat-soluble
Helps: normal blood clotting, normal liver function
Sources: cabbage, cauliflower, soya beans, pork, beef, liver, potatoes,
tomatoes, egg yolk
Depleting factors: air pollution, antibiotics, aspirin, diarrhoea

We do have one word of warning: don't monkey about with your vitamin and mineral intake. The aim in nutrition is to have a sufficiency, not an excess. Just because a substance aids the formation of muscle, for instance, it does not follow that megadosing will form lots of muscle; it might form lots of problems instead. Balance is the keynote, which is why sticking to balanced multi-vitamin supplements is the safest way of taking extra nutrients.

Minerals

Depending on the amount that you sweat during training and racing, minerals and trace elements will need to be replaced. Do not concern yourself too much with sodium chloride (salt) – there is usually more than enough in the foods that we eat – but replacement of other minerals can often be more of a problem. Minerals and trace elements are as vital to health as vitamins, and a deficiency can lead to illness.

The biologically active component of the earth's crust, minerals are not synthesised in the body. They have to be supplied, regularly, in our food, but the soils in which crops are grown and on which animals graze are becoming depleted of their mineral content. Selenium, for instance, has been dubbed 'Europe's missing mineral', since it is present in extremely low levels, if at all, in our soil. Modern growing and farming techniques are not restoring the mineral content, with the result that our food supply is not always a dependable source.

Plants and animals grow well without it, so deficiencies have not yet been noticed, but researchers are now concerned that our reliance on low-selenium wheat means that our prime source of selenium – bread – is no longer dependable. Low selenium levels have been associated with an increased risk of cancer and researchers in New Zealand have found that people with low levels of selenium are more likely to suffer from asthma.

Minerals affect the uptake and absorption of vitamins and can enhance their effects in the body. Minerals are vital components of the chemical catalysts called enzymes without which life itself could not exist. It is important to remember that the action of minerals within the body is interrelated, and one mineral cannot function without affecting – and being affected by – other minerals.

In obvious ways, minerals demonstrate their importance to us: iron enables the blood to transport oxygen; calcium is used to construct bones and teeth; zinc is found in prostatic fluid and semen; potassium and sodium in correct balance are important for the function of cells. Different minerals are absorbed in different ways and many minerals compete with each other for absorption; so it's not enough just to flood your system with minerals. They need to be taken in balance, so don't just pick up on one mineral and start taking extra amounts of it in isolation – take a balanced formula multi-mineral or multi-vitamin and mineral tablet.

MINERAL LIST

Calcium

Function: bone and teeth-building, function of nerves and muscles, blood cholesterol levels and blood clotting, proper tone and elasticity of muscles, including the heart

Magnesium

Function: nerves and muscles associated with calcium metabolism, normal working of the heart, energy production, growth and reproduction of cells

Potassium

Function: regulates balance of water in the body, heart rate, nerve transmission, muscle function, alkalising, helps intestinal tract

Iron

Function: oxygen transport via red blood cells, enzyme component, metabolism of B vitamins

Copper

Function: converts iron, vitamin C metabolism, Depleted by zinc

Chromium

Function: maintenance of blood sugar levels

Selenium

Function: antioxidant enzyme component, works with vitamins E, C and A

Boron

Function: ultra-trace mineral, oestrogen and testosterone levels, calcium and vitamin D associate, connective tissue

Zinc

Function: growth, reproductive system, immune system, wounds and burns, antioxidant enzyme component
Depleted by: smoking, alcohol, contraceptive pills, also lost in perspiration

Manganese

Function: connective tissue such as spinal discs and other cartilages, glucose management.

We need approximately 17 minerals for correct nutrition, and although only 5 per cent of our body weight is accounted for in mineral matter, they are essential for our physical and mental well-being. Not only are they vital factors in maintaining our physiological processes, they also act as catalysts for many biological reactions, including musclular and neural response, the production of hormones and the utilization of nutrients in foods.

Physical and emotional stress can put a strain on our supply of minerals which, along with losses through sweating, can increase our need for mineral intake to exceed more than three times the normal recommended amounts.

Maintaining plasma electrolyte levels in very hot weather can be a problem, due to fluid and mineral salts lost during heavy sweating. Cyclists used to try to overcome this by taking salt tablets. This however was thought to cause high blood pressure in some people, and so was not altogether a satisfactory solution; the electrolyte replacement drinks are better (*see* **Fluid replacement** *page 86*).

Another cause of mineral loss can be caused by our efforts to increase the fibre in our diet. Many cyclists use bran to increase dietary fibre. But all fibre, especially fibre from grains, contains phytic acid which can bind with minerals – particularly iron, calcium and zinc – to form phytates and prevent their absorption. If you are taking a multi-vitamin supplement which also contains minerals or mineral supplements, do not take them at breakfast if you tend to eat whole grain cereals, etc.

Essential fatty acids

Essential fatty acids (EFAs) are an integral component of cell walls, and they can be metabolised to form chemical messengers known as prostaglandins, which run many different metabolic pathways: for example one of the most important of these messengers, prostaglandin E1 (PGE1), is an anti-inflammatory agent, it helps lower blood pressure, reduces the stickiness of platelets in the blood, and can activate T-cells of the immune system; it also helps reduce cholesterol production, balance cell production and can produce effects similar to neuro-transmitters, the brain chemicals associated with mood control.

It is thought that your essential fatty acid levels can affect your general health, so supplements are available to boost your levels and thereby maximise their benefits.

According to Dr Donald Rudin[†], three major developments have disrupted our essential fatty acid balance: flour refining (which removes B vitamins, minerals and essential fatty acids from our normal diet), increasing dependence on high saturated animal fat, and the hydrogenation – literally treatment with hydrogen – of oils that are used for cooking and turn up in margarine, cakes, pastries and other cooked foods.

Hydrogenation is carried out to prevent rancidity. But refining and hydrogenation rob the oils of essential fatty acids, and also create high levels of what Dr Rudin calls 'funny fats'. 'These 'impostor' fatty acids behave like freeloaders, infiltrating cell membranes and stealing enzymes so that real fatty acids can't do their work', he says. This gives us another good reason to supplement our intake.

The most commonly available supplement is Evening Primrose oil. The Evening Primrose plant is one of the richest natural sources of GLA, or gamma-linolenic acid, from which the body produces many vital prostaglandins.

Other sources of fatty acids are blackcurrant oil, Oil of Javanicus by Health and Diet, and 'GLA Forte' by Nutri-Tec. The latter is thought to be of direct benefit to the immune system. Its proportion of saturated, polyunsaturated and monosaturated fats is near the dietary ideal of the World Health Organisation and the United Nations Food and Agriculture Commission. It also supplies squalene, a substance needed for the production of white blood cells.

The latest breakthrough in research on the subject of EFAs suggests that another source is flax seed oil, better known as linseed oil.

Both Dr Donald Rudin and Udo Erasmus[‡] recommend flaxseed/linseed oil as the supplement of the future. But both suggest that there is still an important place for GLA supplements (like Evening Primrose). The body can have difficulties converting essential fatty acids, so using a supplement that helps this process still makes sense. Erasmus says some people take three sources: 'They obtain essential fatty acids from flax for omega-3s and perhaps sunflower or sesame seed oil for omega 6s and take evening primrose oil and fish oil for omega 6 and 3 derivatives, on top of that'.

[†]*'The Omega Three Phenomenon'* by Dr Donald Rudin and Clara Felix, with Constance Schrader, Sigwick and Jackson, 1988

[‡]*'Fats and Oils, the complete guide to fats and oils in health and nutrition'* by Udo Erasmus, available price $14.50 from the Gerson Institute, PO Box 430, Bonita, CA 92002, USA

Enzymes

Without enzymes there would be no life, since enzymes run the body's chemical processes. When the body takes in oxygen and starts to process it, toxins known as 'free radicals' are produced. Enzymes take these free radicals and render them harmless.

Enzymes are easily destroyed in the body, but this is not normally a problem, since we are continually making new ones. However, our capacity to generate enzymes diminishes as we get older, whilst our need for them increases. This is because the free radicals produced by the body's use of oxygen are also produced in large quantities in response to pollution, long-term doses of radiation, poor nutrition (particularly a high intake of processed foods and fats) and − the one that will affect you most − exercise.

Free radicals produced in large amounts stop cells receiving nourishment. When this happens the cell walls thicken and harden. This can result in muscle stiffness and causes friction and heat in the joints after exercise − leading to long-term damage to joints. This may be the mechanism behind arthritis. Possibly one of the greatest advances in sports nutrition is the recent development of tablets of biologically available antioxidant enzymes. The theory behind taking enzymes in tablet form for the sporting cyclist is that they can assist the body's normal enzyme production and 'eat' lactic acid and the waste products of exercise, cutting soreness, stiffness and fatigue.

Britain's toughest stage race was chosen for an experiment to test the new generation of antioxidant enzyme supplements as it is a severe test of stamina, speed − and the ability to come out fighting day after day for three weeks. One of the top professional cyclists in the race was also a sports therapist. After the race he commented: 'The supplements definitely helped. I felt better, and my recovery was better'. In previous races he would normally suffer from extremely tight calves and thighs; a veteran of international stage races, he arranged to have his quadriceps muscles 'stripped' after every day's effort during stage races. This painful massage technique was the only way he could guarantee getting back on the bike the next day; but by taking the supplements regularly, he stayed loose and did not need the treatment at all.

On another occasion, one of us (FW) had been working as soigneur to the Great Britain squad in the Milk Race and the British Cycling Federation had been supplied with vitamins and enzyme supplements for the riders. It was my first experience of the use of enzyme supplementation in a stage race, and I was very impressed when the team came away winning the most stages and most of the prize money; every rider in the team got a stage win.

Our experience there convinced us to that you could race harder and recover more quickly by using supplements; a great asset when riding stage races and long distance events each week.

Following their use on the Milk Race, they were 'road tested' by a selection of people from different sports and at different levels of ability. The reports from coaches and sportspeople are only anecdotal, but they are an indication that enzyme supplements can be used to advantage in longer events.

Let's take enzyme by enzyme the ones shown to be of benefit. *Glutathione peroxidase* removes the free radicals that particularly attack fats. It helps the liver (which is around half fatty tissue) and has been used to treat skin and connective tissue problems. In particular, it is said to be valuable in the collagen diseases, and since

> 'collagen comprises 30 per cent of the body's protein, serving as a major structural component of skin, ligaments, tendons, muscles, cartilage, bones and teeth, glutathione peroxidase is a very important antioxidant enzyme'.
>
> (Dr Linda Lee, Phd)

Superoxide dismustase (SOD) and catalase work together. Research implies that arthritis and other joint problems − sometimes severe enough to put a cyclist out of the sport for good − are not necessarily due to 'over-use' or ageing, but may be caused by a deficiency of SOD/catalase. Having examined the evidence, our view is that supplements of the correct forms of SOD-catalase complex might be able to help cyclists avoid arthritis altogether, despite the hammering they give their joints.

Methionine reductase is the only enzyme known to remove a type of free radical, known as hydroxyl. Hydroxyls are created when we burn fat, and heavy exercise, particularly in a polluted environment, generates hydroxyls.

> 'People using methionine reductase have reported greater endurance, stamina, flexibility and ability to recover from hard workouts'.
>
> (Baranowski and Aydelotte, *A Guide to Cellular Health*)

One of the problems in taking enzyme supplements is that they can be destroyed by digestive acids in the stomach if the tablet is not 'enteric coated' and taken at the correct time. The enteric coating makes the content of the tablet resistant to the acid in the stomach but allows it to easily break down in the alkaline small intestine.

It needs to be said that the supplements will not turn a Sunday biker into a world champion, and although some sports scientists are looking into the effects of enzyme supplementation there have been no trials to prove the efficacy or otherwise of the tablets for the hard training sporting cyclist. However, the evidence so far, albeit empirical, is that they could have a role to play in offsetting the damaging effects of competition, and in helping cyclists of all abilities to avoid training themselves into injury, infection and illness.

Over my years as a sports therapist I (FW) have seen many top sportsmen deprived of the success they deserve when their general health gave way to 'mystery viruses'. So I would urge you to put back into your bodies what the intensive training and competition takes out.

Fluid replacement

Water forms approximately 75% of all protoplasm, and is essential as a medium for various enzyme and chemical reactions, in addition to preventing damage to the organs by diluting the toxic wastes which are a by-product of metabolism. So fluid replacement is of paramount importance, especially during hot weather, when both racing and training. Your thirst, or how wet you are from sweat, are not good indicators of your bodily needs. Drink before you get thirsty, and drink little and often to be safe, especially during hot conditions. On dry, windy days you could be sweating but the body may feel dry as the sweat is quickly evaporating; you'll be dehydrated before you realise it. Drinking is often a matter of habit and you may be one of these disciplined people who limits it to coffee breaks and the like, but during hot weather your fluid requirements increase.

Several electrolyte replacement drinks are now available containing various concentrations of glucose and minerals. Typical of sportsmen, some cyclists work on the principle that if one spoonful is good for you, two is twice as good, which is of course not so. When using these products it is important to mix to the manufacturers' recommendations and then slightly adjust the mix to your personal taste and need, bearing in mind that the more concentrated the mixture the slower the absorption rate from the stomach. Replacement of water is far more important than the replacement of the electrolytes as these can usually be put back after the race or training session by your food.

Check the state of your fluid balance by the colour of your urine. A darker colour indicates a more concentrated urine and the need to take in more fluid. Because of the long distances covered in training and racing, you should ensure that your urine is as clear as water before the race.

> *Don't share your bottle*
>
> Racing cyclists are in the habit of sharing the contents of their water bottle with team-mates, but this practice can be dangerous, particularly for younger riders who may not have fully developed their immune systems. Gastrointestinal infections can easily be passed on in this way. Bear in mind that there are over 70 enteroviruses (gut viruses) that are water-spread and are particularly prevalent in the summer months.

Weight control and performance

Your weight is not that important. You need to know how much of you is muscle and how much is fat.

Recording your weight does not tell you anything about the ratio of fat to lean muscle. Many riders actually gain weight when they start training, because muscular tissue is heavier than fatty tissue, and as you train you tend to exchange fat for muscle. As a result you could feel fitter, even look thinner, but weigh more, and in road, mountain bike and cyclo-cross events you are at a disadvantage if you are carrying excess weight. But it is difficult to assess your body fat levels without expensive tests; optimum weight is an individual matter and reducing your weight below your optimum can lead to loss of strength.

An effective weight is one with a healthy water balance, optimum muscle mass, and no excess body fat (although some body fat is essential to protect the vital organs and energy reserve). If these are out of balance you will experience a drop in your performance. You will find your own individual racing weight, the one at which you perform the best, from experience.

It's quite normal to put on weight during the off season, and provided the increase is not too great this variation can sometimes help the body to recover from the ravages of racing. As you get back into training it will gradually come down, returning to 'racing weight' at the start of the new season.

6   Injuries

No bike-rider ever seems to go through a complete season without having some kind of health problem. Cycling injuries differ from other sports injuries; the occupational hazard of training and racing on roads or across country means that a single fall, crash or collision may cause more damage than another athlete would suffer in an entire career.

It is possible that by training over the long distances for cycle racing we become too used to pain. Quite apart from the physical and mental challenge familiar to every sportsperson, bike-riders also have to adapt to their machines: there is the problem of an unnatural position and the strain on the body of what computer buffs call 'the man-machine interface'. If you are going to get anywhere as a cyclist, you will long ago have realised that you need to adjust to the pain you can experience during training as a matter of routine. Normally this is fine, but there could be the risk that you get out of the habit of 'listening' to your body to pick up those subtle clues that tell the difference between pushing hard to improve performance and going over the brink into injury. Because of the strain of training and racing, even minor health problems can develop into major ones if they aren't handled properly, and a blind faith that they will simply go away or that you can 'ride them out' is not going to ensure that you stay healthy and fit.

Prevention

The most important preventive measure of all is the wearing of protective head gear at all times when bike riding. Most countries now have regulations regarding the use of helmets during road racing, but you would be wise to wear one in time trials, training and social riding: it is possible to incur serious damage to the brain as a result of a fall even at slow speeds.

Many serious injuries can be avoided by experienced racing cyclists by using common sense preventive measures. Skin damage to the body can be reduced by wearing an undervest – in the event of a crash, the surfaces of the vest and racing jersey glide over each other, absorbing some of the friction from the road. Track mitts or gloves reduce damage to the hands, but the unprotected legs can fall victim to some nasty scrapes and infections. Most racing cyclists shave their legs in an effort to reduce possible complications following a crash. Wounds are easier to clean, and sticking plasters are less painful to remove; added to this it is also easier to apply and remove massage oils or pre-race embrocations.

It is very important that you understand what can be done to assist recovery from injury. Most minor injuries sustained through bike riding heal without any medical treatment, but although they may not require treatment they do need watching. For the most part your body is a self-healing, self-repairing mechanism, but sometimes it needs help, especially when you are putting it through a rigorous training programme. 'Treatment' may well come down to removing the obstacles you are putting in the way of the body patching itself up; that may simply mean a day or two of rest. If left completely untreated, a minor injury could become serious and affect your training and racing plans.

Although pain is difficult to define, as the levels experienced differ from person to person, it is said to be nature's way of talking to you; a slight pain can be a warning, whilst a sharp or intense pain can be a shout for help. Nature does not stand still; an injury will improve or deteriorate. In the case of the latter you should seek expert advice. Your doctor should be consulted in all cases of severe joint injuries and any condition that is not showing signs of improvement or causing pain, no matter how slight it seems.

Once when I (FW) was on the Milk Race a rider in another team was involved in a crash. He didn't think it was serious, and did not seek medical attention. Over the following days he had to fight to stay in the race, although he was a rider of some class. Because of his almost instant loss of form he came to ask me what I thought was wrong, and on looking at his injury I discovered that it was infected, and had red streaks affecting his lymph nodes, which were also inflamed. I said that in my opinion he must see the race doctor, abandon the race and go home for rest and medical care. He did not seem too keen on the second part of my advice, but the race doctor, on seeing his condition, withdrew him from the race and sent him home. His team manager was upset at losing such a rider, but had advice been sought earlier he could have recovered to complete the race.

One of the advantages of being fit is that you can often shake off certain ailments quicker than the unfit person. On the other hand, being fit is not the same as being healthy − as a cursory glance at the numbers of superbly fit internationals laid low every year by a 'mystery virus' will prove. You need to protect your health just as you need to train for fitness.

You may find yourself out in all weathers, suffer from fatigue or get involved in a crash: looking after your health will help you through such conditions. Cycle racing has a valid claim to being the world's most demanding sport, and it can put you in line for more trouble than the average person. So let us examine some of the commoner problems that bike-riders face, and consider how best to minimise their adverse effect on your progress.

Injuries: the big three

Cycling injuries fall into three main groups.

1. Direct violence: direct blows, crashing into stationary objects, other vehicles, impact with the ground, etc. Head injuries and broken bones are the most serious consequences, and there are likely to be torn tissues, bruising and inflammation.

2. Indirect violence: a sudden strain of some sort, usually opposing muscles, causing a pull or sprain, for example, twisting a muscle as in a fall or in an attempt to keep your balance. All the muscle tears of every type including, unusually, a tear in the middle − more likely to happen to trained bike riders than untrained ones − are in this category. Untrained bikers are prone to get their tears at the origin or insertion of a muscle, where it comes off the bone, or in the muscle tendon; so as well as torn tissues you get bruising and inflammation.

3. Over-use: probably the commonest of all cycle sport injuries. Cyclists are keen trainers and take their bodies to the limit of endurance in training and racing. Some riders' tissues just won't stand up to that amount of punishment: the result is over-use injury.

What to do first

In the majority of cycle sport injuries, the first and best treatment to aid your recovery is RICE:

R − rest

I − ice

C − compression

E − elevation

Rest, to avoid possible further injury and promote healing.
Ice, to constrict the blood vessels, reduce pain and stop further internal bleeding.
Compression, to help reduce swelling. Following an injury, blood and fluid will often accumulate in the damaged area. Left uncontrolled, the swelling would create greater pain and prolong recovery time.
Elevation, to use gravity to help drain excess fluids from the injured area.

You should use RICE as soon as possible, as swelling can often start within seconds of the injury. Don't apply ice directly to the skin as it can cause damage. Instead, get crushed or cubed ice, or an ice pack, and wrap it in a wet cloth or towel, then apply it. In extremely cold conditions, use a dry cloth or towel to avoid possible frostbite.

For compression, use an elastic bandage, taking care not to apply it too tightly and cut off your blood supply. If you feel tingling or numbness, check the bandage. Although these sensations can be created by the ice, they must not be ignored. It is always a good practice to check your pulse after applying the compress.

The cold pack must only be in place for 20-30 minutes, no longer. On removal, reapply the compression bandage and elevate the limb. After about 90 minutes the cold pack should be reapplied and the whole procedure repeated twice or three times a day for the next two days.

Cold therapy may cause the following reactions: cold, tingling, aching, burning or numbness; the pack should still be left in place throughout any of these stages. These reactions are almost always due to the cold pack, but stay aware and keep checking that you have not unwittingly applied a tourniquet to yourself or have burnt yourself with the ice.

Don't use RICE where there is a history of any circulatory condition, serious open wounds, or if a fracture is suspected. Limbs should not be moved or elevated without first being splinted, if a fracture is suspected.

Massage with ice

* Fill a polystyrene cup with water and freeze. Trim an inch or so of the foam from the top so the ice protrudes. Cover the skin of the area to be treated with a film of body oil or Vaseline to prevent the possibility of an ice burn.
* Apply the ice to the area to be treated, moving in firm circular movements over a slightly wider area than the injury.
* Period of treatment should not exceed 10 minutes.
* Ice massage stimulates the deep circulation and slightly anaesthetises the area, so that gentle stretching can be performed without pain.

Cold water packs for healing

The first effect of a cold water treatment is that the skin is chilled and blood is driven to the deeper tissues. Then a reaction takes place: the superficial blood vessels (capillaries) dilate and the blood returns to the surface. The sudden application of cold water to the surface of the body arouses and stimulates the circulation all over the system. It also deepens respiration, and these two effects account for the tonic effect of cold water applications. A pack consists of a cloth or sheet soaked in cold water, thoroughly wrung out and wrapped snugly around and over the injured area. It must always be covered with an outer blanket, wrapped so it excludes air. The inner cloth may be of linen or cotton and should be wrung practically dry before being applied. After a few minutes' contact with the body, the pack becomes warm and there is a reduction in the temperature of the injured area. Most people think that the packs reduce the temperature because they are put on cold. This is not how they work, and if the pack stays cold then it is not being applied correctly, or you are not raising the right response to it. The coldness of the pack may lower the surface temperature slightly, but it is the moist warmth forming under the pack on the surface of the body that draws the blood from the congested deep tissues to the skin, which relaxes and opens the pores and in that way helps heat to escape from the body.

A pack for the whole body

For a body pack you need a cotton or linen sheet and two or more blankets spread in order of weight (heaviest first) on a bed.

∗ On the top blanket spread the linen or cotton sheet, which has been dipped into cold water and wrung out fairly dry. Let the blankets extend about one foot beyond the wet sheet at the head of the bed.
∗ Lie down on the wet sheet so that it comes well up to your neck and wrap it snugly around your body so that it covers every part, except the feet, tucking it in between your arms and sides and between your legs. You need help for this − otherwise make sure you leave one arm free!
∗ The blankets are then folded, one by one, upwards around the feet and around the body, turned in at the neck and brought across the chest. The feet must be kept warm during the entire treatment − you may need to apply hot water bottles.
∗ Stay wrapped in the body pack from one to two hours according to the severity of the injury and your reaction to the pack.

For a leg or arm pack, wring out a smaller piece of linen or cotton sheet with cold water and wrap snugly around the arm or leg, covering the limb completely. Then cover completely with a flannel sheet or blanket and safety pin in position. Leave on for between one and two hours. After you've taken off the pack, shower or sponge area to clean off the secretions removed from the skin by sweating.

The leg and arm pack is very valuable in relieving inflammation, and is most beneficial for aching legs after a long hard race.

Shock

Shock is always a possibility in any crash injury, but in the event of a fracture or deep wound with severe bleeding shock is almost certain to develop. It may be that you are first on the scene when there has been a serious accident, so it would be as well to know how to recognise it and what to do about it.

The most important indicator of potential shock is the degree of injury; the injured person may lapse into a state of shock without showing any of the usual signs or symptoms, so assume that shock is present in all cases of severe injury. Extreme conditions − extreme exposure to heat or cold, or severe dehydration or fatigue − can also predispose the injured cyclist to shock. The level of primary shock is dependent on the nature of the injury, and the age and physical condition of the casualty.

Symptoms of shock

* Breathing shallow and rapid
* Colour usually pale
* Pulse fast, tending to become weak
* Touch cold and clammy
* Faintness
* Giddiness
* Nausea

Treatment for primary shock

Place casualty in appropriate position, i.e. lying down, head low, legs raised about 8-12 inches (although of course the initial positioning will vary according to the type of injury. If a leg fracture is suspected, then the leg should be kept level until splinted).

If the victim is unconscious, seems likely to vomit, or has difficulty breathing, place him in the recovery position. If he has suffered a heart attack, sit him down or place him in a recumbent position. Loosen tight clothing and maintain body warmth (but do not overheat). **Treat urgently the cause of the shock.** Comfort and reassure the casualty, but do not give anything to eat or drink, or allow the casualty to smoke.

Diagnosis

Bike riding injuries usually involve damage to the seven main tissue structures − skin, muscles, tendons, ligaments, fasciae, bones and joints.

Damage to the skin is visible, so it is easier to assess. Diagnosis of deeper tissue damage requires some knowledge of anatomy, but it's not always very mysterious. You can often feel or sense what structures are involved. The pain felt when moving your knee after a crash will tell you straight away that you have done some damage to the joint, even though you do not have a medical degree. Likewise, if a muscle is tender to move or touch, you will realise that you have a muscle injury. In many cases, however, it's the *degree* of injury that will determine whether you can treat yourself, and that's not always obvious. Never hesitate to get a qualified medical opinion on an injury. Symptoms of shock, intense pain, or feelings of weakness or illness should be taken as signals to get yourself to a doctor as soon as possible. Equally, don't exclude the possibility of helping yourself. Taking the correct action while an injury is 'fresh' can often stop minor problems becoming serious: this is the

basis of all first aid. Don't resist professional help or first aid on the grounds that people involved with a tough sport shouldn't need it. Every successful athlete these days has access to reliable, experienced help. You are subjecting yourself to greater stress than the average person, and you may need medical support.

Antibiotics

A regular treatment for all kinds of infections, antibiotics need to be properly understood. They can be lifesavers, but people do use them for conditions that would be better treated by letting the body build up its own powers of resistance, rather than by relying on repeated doses of drugs. This advice does not necessarily apply to you, however, as competitive cyclists are already under stress, and you may well need a course of antibiotics to clear up an infection.

Antibiotics work by attacking bacterial infections in your system. The symptoms may disappear before the infection is completely eradicated, but if you stop taking the antibiotics the symptoms may return. So the first rule, if you are prescribed antibiotics, is to take the complete course: resist the temptation to stop the medication because you feel better.

If you are against the idea of taking drugs, then there are alternative treatments you can use, bearing in mind that you can always use antibiotics if these fail. One of the most powerful broad-spectrum natural antibiotics is garlic. It acts against bacteria, viruses and fungi, and is thought to be even more effective against certain micro-organisms than drugs. You can add fresh garlic to your daily food or, if you don't like the smell or the taste, use a quality garlic supplement (from health food shops or pharmacists). This should be a type that has its smell factor intact, as research shows the chemical that gives the smell is one of garlic's most powerful constituents. Slices of raw garlic can also be used on skin infections, not only for its antibiotic effect but because it can stimulate the growth of new tissue.

Antibiotics may interact with nutritional supplements you might be taking for other reasons. If you are taking any iron or mineral supplements, stop them during your antibiotics course. Once it is completed, resume them, preferably as part of a general multi-nutrient plus iron supplementation course. Some antibiotics, particularly the oxytetracycline types, interact with dairy products, which reduces their absorption into the system. So it is best to cut down on milk, butter and cheese foods during a course of antibiotics.

One undesirable effect of antibiotics is that they kill off some of the body's natural, beneficial bacteria as well as the harmful ones. As a result, body toxins may build up, so it is a good idea to increase your intake of vitamin C during the course (but not dosing at the same time of day as the antibiotics). After taking antibiotics, it is helpful to encourage the beneficial bacteria to 'repopulate' by eating natural live yoghurt.

The way back

The speed and success of your recovery from an injury will depend on several factors. It starts with your primary care: did you do the RICE treatment? Another factor is the gravity of the injury: the more serious the injury, the longer it will take to repair. If you are fit and healthy your rate of repair will be rapid, but many a fast recovery has been ruined by impatience to return to racing. Another factor often not considered is age: the older you are, the longer you must allow for the healing processes to do their work.

Listen to your body. When your injury stops hurting at rest, start gentle movements. If there is no pain, do gentle stretching and maybe a light session on the turbo trainer. This routine can be increased gradually so long as there is no pain. If the pain returns, you have overdone it and you need to cut down to a pain- free level of activity. If you have a leg injury you could do upper body development, and vice versa.

What to do for: a guide to first aid and injuries

A – Z of health problems

Health problems that can arise from bike riding and hard training can very often be dealt with by yourself. In the following injuries guide we have put our suggestions for self treatment under the heading 'self help'. Although self help will often bring relief there are times when medical help is essential – so bear in mind that the condition must always show a steady improvement. Any lack of progress or a deterioration in the condition is an indication that a visit to your doctor is required.

Athlete's foot

A contagious fungal infection with the impressive name of tinea pedis. It usually affects the first layer of skin between the toes, but can also affect the toe-nails.

This ringworm-type infection can also affect other parts of the body and could seriously impede training and racing if the groin area is infected (tinea curis). Although this condition can cure itself in time, it is best not to ignore it as it can also get worse.

Signs and symptoms

Dead moist skin with a musty odour and itching in the inflamed areas between the toes, making you want to keep scratching, sometimes to the point of bleeding.

Treatment

Usually only required if the condition is really serious. You may then be prescribed an oral anti-fungal medication.

Self help

Wash the feet thoroughly every day to remove the scales and matter between the toes. Dry well and apply non-prescription anti-fungal powders or creams.

Garlic is probably nature's most powerful anti-fungal; it can be taken orally or, even better, fresh garlic can be rubbed on the affected areas. Aromatherapists sometimes recommend tea tree oil as an anti-fungal measure. The homoeopathic remedy Sepia 30x taken daily for a week can also be of help.

Prevention

Prevention is better than cure, so look to your personal hygiene. Always wash your feet after any training and racing. Dry well especially between the toes. If your feet tend to get very hot and sweaty when training, use a foot powder or menthol cream and let the air get to your feet whenever possible by wearing open sandals, without socks, about the house.

See your doctor . . .

. . . if you have severe persistent symptoms, or if it seems to be spreading despite your self help measures.

Back pain

Pain in the lower back goes with the territory as far as many cyclists are concerned, but then most of them don't have a regular stretching routine.

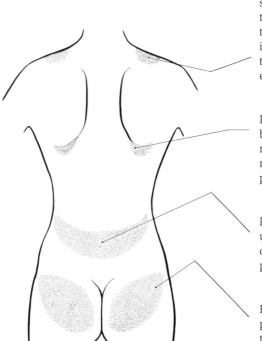

Pain in this area often occurs at the start of the season, following long training rides wearing scarves or track suits with high necks, and is often caused by the neck having to push against the resistance of the extra clothing.

Pain at the base of the shoulder blades can be due to incorrect riding position, or using tri-bars in races without getting used to the position in training.

Lumbar pain is often caused by undergoing long, hilly training rides or races without correct build-up preparation.

Hip/gluteal pain can follow from prolonged hard efforts, such as a time trial on a very windy day.

Signs and symptoms

Prolapsed discs and similar problems need diagnosis by a chiropractor, osteopath or doctor. But many of the nagging back problems suffered by cyclists are simply caused by tension in the lower back muscles. The basic racing position on the bicycle, coupled with the way we use our backs under effort, produces tension in the hip and low back region.

It usually starts with an ache in the lumbar region and in the deep part of the buttock. This ache is in the muscles used for driving round the pedals, and they are especially stressed when big gears are used.

The pain can be brought on suddenly by indecision when riding in a group. A rider attacks; you wonder whether to jump in pursuit, and you start to make the effort while your muscles are tense. When the effort is over, sometimes the muscles stay contracted, which puts pressure on the various nerve sources around the muscles – and you get backache. Usually you can ease this by stretching. Lie on your back; bring your knees up into your chest and your head down to meet your knees. (*See* **Stretching exercise 19** *page 64*) This exercise can be incorporated into your daily stretching routine as a guard against backache. If the condition does not ease with stretching, then it pays to visit a qualified practitioner for treatment.

Treatment

If you have pain you can take painkillers such as paracetamol or aspirin but remember these are not tackling the condition.

Self help

RICE for 48 hours, then use heat or ice massage three or four times a day for not longer than ten minutes at a time. Elevation might be a little difficult! Instead emphasise the rest.

Vitamin C is vital for the health and maintenance of connective tissue, which is entirely what a spinal disc is made from.

See your doctor . . .

. . . if any back pain is intense.

Blisters

Fluid under the top layer of skin.

Signs and symptoms

Sensitivity to pressure with redness and swelling.

Treatment

Only required if infected.

Self help

Where possible, blisters should be protected by a dressing but usually if you leave them alone the fluid will be reabsorbed. If the blister is painful it may help to pierce it. To do this apply ice for five minutes, wash with soap and water, dry the area using clean cotton wool and puncture the blister several times around the edge with a sterilized needle (to sterilize boil it in water for 10 minutes), leave the skin in place and apply gentle pressure to squeeze out the fluid, cover with gauze and moleskin. (Moleskin is a thin protective adhesive plaster available at most chemists.)

Prevention and training   If it is your feet that are particularly prone to blisters, use good shoes that fit well, with no raised seams on the inside. Tape or apply moleskin to the toes or other vulnerable areas before training or racing. In wet weather, lightly grease toes with vaseline. By following these directions your training and racing should not be impeded.

See your doctor . . .   . . . if the blister is still painful despite treatment, or if there are signs of infection.

Bruises   Haematoma, or bruising, is one of the most obvious of a bike-rider's battle scars. A bruise is caused by bleeding inside the tissues. If you just get a knock you may get a small bruise. If you get a bruise of any size, it must mean damage to tissue, because you have broken blood vessels. If there is a lot of bruising, then there has been quite gross tissue damage; you must have torn a structure, or could even have sustained a fracture, and this will require medical attention.

A bruise may not always be on the site of an injury. Any blow to the lower leg, for instance, may result in a bruise right down at the ankle, because the blood will run along the fascial planes – the sheets of membranes and connective tissue. So where the bruise comes out is not necessarily where the damaged tissue is, even though the site of the bruise may be sore. This sensitivity is usually caused by the seeping blood irritating the surrounding tissue. So you always get some inflammation with a bruise, which is what makes it painful. Other body fluids can also cause pain: there is synovial fluid in our joints, and a leak into the tissues can cause a lot of irritation. The whole calf can swell up if you have damage to the knee joint; this can create a painful calf muscle, when the real problem is the knee. (*See* **knee problems** *page 116*.)

Treatment   Ibuprofen is helpful and if the condition is very inflamed your doctor will prescribe non-steroid anti-inflammatory drugs.

Self help   If you have a tendency to bruise easily, you might be helped by extra vitamin C and bioflavonoids, the naturally occurring substances that always accompany vitamin C in foods. The homoeopathic remedy arnica is also useful for bruising (and bleeding) after an injury.

Externally, witch-hazel, comfrey or calendula, applied on a compress or simply smeared lightly on a bruise can all help the healing process.

See your doctor . . .   . . . if you see a lot of bruising. You may also have a lot of discomfort; ask for an X-ray as the condition could be due to a fracture.

Boils	An infection, usually staphylococcus bacteria, of the hair follicle.
Signs and symptoms	A painful, tender, raised area with pus at the surface. Boils often appear quite suddenly and ripen in 24 hours. Sometimes swelling of the closest lymph glands.
Treatment	If self help treatment does not solve the problem, incision and drainage of the boil by a doctor may be necessary, and a course of antibiotics.
Self help	In most cases it is better to encourage a boil to burst by poulticing it twice daily with cotton wool or gauze soaked in hot water, Calendula lotion or Hypercal tincture. Wrap the gauze around the end of a wooden spoon, wet the gauze in the lotion and gently apply the moist hot poultice to the boil, taking care not to scald yourself with a poultice that is too hot. Continue for up to five minutes, refreshing the poultice frequently in the hot lotion. Rinse with cold water, then dress the boil with gauze and magnesium sulphate paste or suitable drawing ointment, which you can get from your local health shop or pharmacy.
	Boils are common and contagious; prevent them spreading by using only clean towels or paper towels.
Training	Although boils can develop in many areas, the bike rider usually gets them at the point of contact with the saddle. Boils are very painful and make it impossible to sit in the saddle properly, so it is better to maintain your heart-lung fitness by running or swimming until they have healed.
See your doctor . . .	. . . if new boils develop or symptoms don't improve in three to four days despite treatment.
Bronchitis	Bronchitis is an inflammation of the bronchial tubes, but often the infection affects the nose, throat and air passages in the lungs. Cyclists are vulnerable to bronchitis because they train and race in all kinds of conditions.
	Do not train while you have bronchitis − go and see your doctor.
Signs and symptoms	The symptoms include a persistent cough, with or without mucus. In more advanced cases your breathing can become difficult and painful, and if you don't seek treatment you may sustain permanent lung damage.
Treatment	If you have had repeated chest colds, go to your doctor.

Self help

Do not train while you have bronchitis. Stay indoors, take vitamin C, and use inhalations. These inhalations should be of Olbas Oil (a blend of natural oils which has many healthy uses for the cyclist) or of Bengue's Balsam. Have a bowl of very hot water, with either a few drops of Olbas Oil or about an inch of Bengue's Balsam dissolved into it. Put a towel over your head and gently inhale the vapours. Do this several times per day.

Training

All training must stop. If you go training with bronchitis you will only make it worse. Make no mistake, bronchitis is a very serious condition.

See your doctor . . .

. . . if you think you have bronchitis, you must see your doctor.

Colds

Cyclists tend to get more than their fair share of the common cold − a viral infection of the respiratory system, affecting the nose, throat and bronchi in particular.

You may have to face them every year, but, taking them up the road and 'riding them out of your system' is not the answer. That is an old idea now regarded as potentially dangerous.

If neglected, colds can be dangerous, but you can normally deal with them yourself if you act promptly when they start. Take normal common sense precautions: stay indoors in the warm, keep your body temperature up, take plenty of fluids and get plenty of rest.

Signs and symptoms

Symptoms usually appear 24-48 hours after infection and may include: blocked-up nose, runny nose, reduction in the sense of smell and taste, headache, shivering, sore throat, cough, feeling of listlessness.

Treatment

Not usually required at the onset of a cold, but can be essential if self care is neglected.

Although antibiotics are not effective in treating viral conditions they may be prescribed to avoid other possible infections.

Self help

Take two garlic capsules twice a day for the duration of the cold. Olbas Oil inhalations will also help to make you feel more comfortable. Although the thought of using a cold body pack does not appeal to everybody, it will help your body detoxify.

There are several non-prescriptive preparations on the market, but be very careful what you decide to take and be absolutely sure it is not on the proscribed list. (*See* **Banned substances** *page 138.*) The recommended way to speed the cold on its way without the worry of dope tests would be to take two water-soluble aspirins every four hours during the day (up to a maximum of eight tablets a day), alternating with one gram of vitamin C in effervescent tablet form every four hours. So the two hourly dosage would be alternately aspirin, vitamin, aspirin, vitamin, and so on. Halfway through the first day you will be feeling worse, but as the day continues you will feel much, much better. It is sometimes possible, using this method, to clear a cold up within a day.

If you are not in a rush, it is better to let the cold run its course and accept the cue to take it easy for a while. Take vitamin C, eat lightly or just drink light soups and rest.

See your doctor . . .

. . . if the condition does not improve with self-help. Colds should only last a day or two anyway. If a cold lingers on it is probably because you don't have the vitality to throw it off – as children normally do. One solution is to see a doctor; the other is to take notice of the message: you may be run down, over-training, or too stressed to heal properly. The answer then is not medication, but some changes to your programme, rest, relaxation and supportive nutrition.

Coughs and sore throats

(*See also* **Colds** *and* **Bronchitis**.)
These are often caused by having to gulp down a lot of cold air – a typical situation in racing or training. The consequent drying out of the back of the throat starts an irritation and a cough.

Signs and symptoms

Swollen glands can often be felt on each side of your windpipe when you have a sore throat or a cold. They usually subside within a day or two, except in children who come into contact with new microbes more often than adults and may go on making antibodies for several weeks. If they appear relatively well despite their enlarged glands, you need not worry for at least a month. But see your doctor if the swelling does not subside.

Treatment

If you are bringing up highly-coloured mucus, then you should go to the doctor; but if the product of your cough is white, you can usually take an expectorant to help it on its way. The only time to take a cough suppressant is if cold air makes your throat irritable and you are coughing without producing mucus.

Bear in mind that many cough mixtures contain banned substances which will certainly be detected in a dope test.

Self help

Sore throats can be treated by gargling with salt water, or water containing soluble aspirin or two drops of Olbas Oil. If you have a slight temperature, the aspirin/vitamin C procedure will often clear it up; but if it persists for more than a week, see your doctor.

Lozenges containing the mineral zinc and vitamin C are a handy and natural preventive treatment (from health foods shops). Research has proved that the zinc inactivates viruses lurking in your throat.

If you don't mind the smell, then include garlic in your food. It has anti-viral and healing properties. If you don't like the taste take a garlic supplement.

Essential oils such as lavender and tea tree oil are also effective natural remedies.

An effective alternative treatment to cough mixtures to ease a sore throat or an unproductive cough is a mixture of glycerin, lemon and honey. This can be bought from any chemist, or made yourself, with a teaspoon each of honey and glycerin, plus the juice of a lemon, mixed with some water. Sip it slowly. It is quite a pleasant way of easing your problem.

See your doctor . . .   . . . if the condition persists or deteriorates despite self-help.

Collarbone (clavicle) fracture   A complete or incomplete break of the clavicle (collarbone); the most common fracture in cycling, caused by taking a fall on an outstretched arm.

Signs and symptoms   Severe pain, swelling and tender to touch at the site of the fracture. Visible deformity if the fracture is complete. Numbness or coldness in the shoulder and arm may be felt on the affected side if the blood supply is impaired.

Treatment   Doctor's diagnosis and treatment may include resetting the bone and putting the arm in a sling or collar and cuff support. Pain killers if required.

Self help   Apply an ice pack to the site of the fracture. After medical treatment, you may use frequent ice massage as a follow up self care.

Take arnica tablets as a homoeopathic remedy for shock and keep warm with blankets, if possible don't move the injured area to remove clothing.

Immobilize the injured area with a sling to reduce the possibility of further damage.

Try to maintain shoulder and hand mobility. Supporting the elbow on injured side with your opposite hand, wave forearm from side to side.

The herb comfrey helps to speed up the work of the white blood cells that are involved in healing, without any loss to their efficiency. The use of comfrey (traditionally known as 'knit-bone') can reduce the healing time by as much as 30%. Use six 400mg tablets of the dessicated root daily for six of the six to eight weeks for the bones to knit. Comfrey is effective, but contains a trace of toxic alkaloid chemical that accumulates in your body, so it is better to avoid using it for longer than four to six weeks at a time.

It might help to take a vitamin C supplement of 100mg with every dose of comfrey tea or tablets, since your white blood cells will need more than usual. Take B complex vitamins as your need may increase to combat the trauma of breaking a bone.

During recovery increase fibre and fluid intake to prevent the constipation that may result from reduced activity.

Training

Stop road or cross-country training for about four weeks, then light road riding might be possible.

Use a turbo trainer one-handed: light riding without pain.

Develop a general stretch and exercise programme.

See your doctor . . .

. . . if there is increased pain, swelling, signs of infection, change in the skin colour or loss of feeling on the injured side.

Cramp

(*See also* **Muscles** *page 120.*)

Cramp is caused when your muscles go into sustained contraction: they shorten as the effort is made, and they stay at their shortest, giving a sharp pain that cannot be ignored. It can last a few seconds or a few minutes, depending on how unlucky you are.

There are several causes of cramp: mineral deficiencies, calling on your muscles to do more than they are accustomed to; hyperventilation; awkward positioning on the bike. Bike-riders usually get cramp because their muscles are being called upon to perform beyond their level of training.

Treatment

You do not usually need medication for this condition.

A typical problem area with cyclists is the large muscle mass of the calf. You should press fairly firmly with your thumb into the thickest part of the muscle and hold for a count of ten. As you put the pressure on, you will feel the cramp gradually easing. This is the best remedy. Another method is to put the affected muscle into the stretch position which is temporarily quite painful because it works against the contracting action of the cramp. A third solution is to use a proprietary cold spray.

If you know that the cramp is due to loss of mineral salts through excess sweating, then a quick remedy is to down one of the commercial electrolyte-replacement drinks. These are intended to replace the various body salts in a balanced way.

On no account take salt tablets, since normal sodium chloride (table-salt) is present in so many foods that you are highly unlikely to be deficient. The most likely deficiencies among body salts are of potassium and magnesium, and it is very easy to keep these in balance by drinking fruit juices. No tablets are needed.

Dehydration

The loss of water and essential body salts as a result of excessive sweating while racing or training on hot weather. It can also be brought on by kidney disease, use of diuretics and loss of fluids through vomiting, fever or diarrhoea.

Signs and symptoms

Reduced or complete lack of urination. Wrinkled skin, low blood pressure and possible coma.

Treatment

Only usually required if self care does not improve condition.

Self help

Condition can be avoided by drinking water frequently in small quantities during racing or training. During hot periods weigh yourself at the same time each day to be aware of possible fluid loss.

Avoid alcohol, drink frequent small amounts of water (avoid drinking large amounts as it may cause vomiting).

Diabetes

Diabetes mellitus is a complex disease involving carbohydrate metabolism, which can be hereditary or developmental. Insufficient insulin or a decrease in the effectiveness of insulin being produced, is usually responsible.

Whether or not diabetes runs in your family, it is wise to protect your health with a diet which excludes, where possible, refined flour, sugar and all manufactured and refined foods containing it. Food additives hidden behind E numbers or very small print on the contents label need to be checked. Some food manufacturers try to make an asset of additives by calling them 'energy-giving', but such additives as sucrose, sugar, glucose, dried glucose syrup, dextrose, fructose, maltose, lactose and so on are highly concentrated forms of sugar often used in huge amounts, and they may well stress the systems of your body which is designed to process more naturally packaged sugars. They are best avoided as your main energy source. It is better to help your health and fitness by eating good 'whole' energy foods containing both fibre and the nutrients you need to metabolise sugar. For example, eat whole wheat, wheat germ and bran containing chromium and manganese, both vital to the health of your pancreas. Raw carrot and onion eaten regularly would also be beneficial for their noted anti-diabetic properties.

Until recent years diabetes sufferers were usually discouraged from participating in competitive sports, but greater knowledge of the condition and improvements in insulin administration has removed most of the objections. In fact a physical fitness programme, such as cycling, can definitely help in the management of the condition. However, control of the condition in racing and training is a very complex subject and the cooperation of a diabetic clinic, along with regular monitoring of your own blood sugar levels, are important precautions against complications.

The control of blood sugars is the key to being able to compete, and the insulin-dependent racing cyclist must constantly monitor his or her intake of food and insulin and the amount of exercise to maintain the correct level of blood sugar. Eat before training or racing, and in long distance events 'top up' with glucose supplements. You may not need to change your insulin dosage, but food intake needs to be increased.

Prevention is better than cure; if you have a family history of diabetes, eating a sensible diet and supplementing this with a good quality chromium supplement, with manganese, may help you to avoid being a diabetic. Your doctor or diabetic clinic can best advise on your needs.

As with all systemic conditions, there are many variables in the insulin-dependent racing cyclist's response to training but if you discuss the problem with your doctor and coach there is usually no reason why you cannot enjoy a full and successful cycle racing career.

Diabetic coma

A dangerous condition. It is brought on by excessive urination, which creates an imbalance of electrolytes, a condition known as ketoacidosis, which can lead to a coma. Early detection of ketoacidosis is essential.

Signs and symptoms

Symptoms, which usually come on slowly, are nausea and vomiting, laboured breathing, sweet, fruity smelling breath. Dry mucus lining of the mouth with thirst and flushed skin. Disorientation or unconsciousness, that can lead to a coma.

Treatment	Medical attention should be sought immediately.
Self help	If you are the victim you are only in a position to help yourself in the early stage: an insulin injection will normally prevent a coma. To help another person, the early detection of ketoacidosis is essential. The patient should be taken to the nearest hospital or doctor as soon as possible.
Training	Your training and racing programme will need to be reassessed.
See your doctor . . .	. . . after emergency treatment, for further advice.

Insulin shock	The opposite to a diabetic coma, this is the reaction when too much insulin is taken into the body, resulting in hypoglycemia (low blood sugar).
Signs and symptoms	Usually comes on rapidly, though there may be initial signs of agitation and confusion along with moist, pale skin, and shallow breathing.
Treatment	Only usually required in severe cases or where the condition does not readily respond to self treatment.
Self help	Most diabetic cyclists carry some lumps of sugar or a chocolate bar in case of need. Cycle training and racing metabolises large amounts of glycogen and the cyclist could, and sometimes does, inadvertently take too much insulin, causing a severe shock reaction. It cannot be stressed too strongly that competitive sportspeople need to monitor their blood sugar levels several times daily to balance their insulin requirements.
Training	Greater attention to your food intake is needed before training and subsequent 'topping up' during the ride.
See your doctor . . .	. . . if the condition regularly returns.

Diarrhoea	Diarrhoea is abnormal stool looseness or even liquid stools. The cause may be difficult to establish as it can be the result of a number of things including emotional upset, viral infection, change of diet, or infestation by parasitic organisms. The pattern of bowel disturbance is a great help in providing a clue to the cause and hence the treatment.

A major problem for the racing cyclist is fluid loss. If you are unlucky enough to fall victim to an attack of infective diarrhoea during a stage race you run the risk of becoming dehydrated, and would be well advised to retire, recover and come back fighting!

Signs and symptoms

Frequent elimination of stools, abdominal cramps, weakness, nausea and sometimes vomiting and fever.

Treatment

During a stage race, the race doctor should always be consulted and the appropriate treatment will be given.

Self help

Drink plenty of fluid, including electrolyte replacement drinks, and keep treatment simple wherever possible. Taking too many medications can further irritate the condition. Self-help medication can be difficult: check that what you intend to take is not on the banned list of substances.

Peppermint essence is good for mild digestive upsets, take 2-10 drops every 2-3 hours. To aid recovery avoid any food that may irritate the digestive system, such as spicy or greasy dishes. Eat bland foods until the symptoms have gone.

Prevention

When travelling abroad to compete, especially for the first time, digestive upsets can arise from jet-lag, excitement or the change of diet. Avoid local tap water, unwashed fruit and vegetables; also iced drinks and ice-cream. Be very thorough in your personal hygiene.

Training

Training should not be attempted once you realise you have this condition; but it can be gradually resumed when you are back to normal. Build your training up slowly, and initially maintain a high fluid intake.

See your doctor . . .

. . . if there is blood in motions, greasy motions, persistent weight loss, abdominal swelling or persistent nausea.

Also see your doctor if you plan to travel in Mediterranean, third world or primitive countries.

Ears

A build up of wax, impaired hearing or ear pain can affect the ears in any sport and cycling is no exception.

Treatment

The ears are very delicate and need to be treated with great care. Any problems that arise must be treated by your doctor. Resist the temptation to attack the wax with matchsticks or anything else. It is surprising how easily your ears can be damaged, and trying to coax the wax out with cotton wool tipped sticks can just help to tamp the wax in more thoroughly. When this happens no air can get in to vibrate the ear drum and you may find yourself going deaf in one or both ears – not only uncomfortable, but dangerous, when survival on the roads is at stake.

Far better to visit your doctor and arrange to have your ears syringed out. You may need to soften up the wax by placing a few drops of olive oil in the ear, morning and evening for two or three days, first.

Excessive ear wax can be just one of those things that some people are more prone to than others. Alternatively what feels like a blockage can actually be due to an infection (a common complaint of serious swimmers).

See your doctor ...   ... in all cases of ear problems.

Eyes   Your eyes need care. They can get very sore, especially in rain or wind, and sore eyes can soon become a problem if neglected.

Signs and symptoms   Eyes are red rimmed and sore – can be itchy.

Treatment   Not usually required in mild cases, but essential in very inflamed conditions or where the soreness is due to a foreign body in the eye that cannot easily be removed.

Self-help   Try not to rub them, especially with gritty fingers – or even worse – fingers covered with embrocation (which can be dangerous).

If you do come in from a dusty or windy ride, use an eye bath and solution. If you use an eye lotion from the chemist, buy small bottles as the shelf life is short once opened. Do not use more than four weeks after opening to be on the safe side and to guard against possible bacterial contamination.

A soothing herbal treatment to ease strained eyes is Euphrasia, or eyebright. An eye bath can be made with drops of Euphrasia tincture in sterile (boiled) cold water, or it can be used in cold pads of cotton wool placed over the eyes.

Prevention   The use of protective eyewear is a good idea. Good cycle shops and opticians stock several designs of cycling glasses, many with interchangeable coloured lenses. The use of these new designs helps to avoid eye strain and keeps out particles of road and country dirt.

See your doctor or optician . . .	. . . if you have any unusual or persistent problems with your eyes.

Exercise-induced bronchospasm (asthma attack)

This condition affects many sporting cyclists, particularly the talented ones. It is a chronic breathing disorder with shortness of breath and wheezing caused by a spasm of the air passage, closing off air to the lungs. Many of the causes are still unknown. There is usually a family history of asthma or allergies, and it may be triggered off by the use of medication that creates an allergic reaction; stress, lung infections and exercising in certain conditions to which you are sensitive.

Signs and symptoms

Tight chest, difficulty in breathing creating a wheezing sound when exhaling. Rapid, shallow breathing with an inability to take in enough air, causing great distress. An attack can deteriorate to a level where you are fighting for air, unable to speak, and your skin takes on a bluish colour.

Treatment

Most asthmatics are already under medical care and have the appropriate medication handy. In the event of a severe attack the person should be taken to hospital as **soon** as possible − delay could be dangerous.

Self help

Sit upright during attacks. Practise deep breathing and relaxation techniques, and try to identify your particular allergens and irritants.

Talk to your doctor about emergency drugs and keep the medication with you at all times.

Training

It is not possible to outline suitable training for this condition because of the multiple causes. If the trigger is stress then cycling will help, but no racing for a while. This condition can often attack the talented rider who is reacting to the stress of improving performances, possible international selection and so on. Take it easy!

See your doctor . . .

. . . if you have frequent asthma attacks or an attack that does not respond to treatment, or if you have any side effects to the prescribed medicine. Check that the medication prescribed is not on the list of banned substances.

Fingertip injury

Injury to fingertips can often result from a crash.

Signs and symptoms

Pain and bleeding. Part of the fingertip may be torn away.

Treatment	Only usually required if injury is serious.
Self help	Plunge injured hand into very cold water washing off any dirt or grit with homoeopathic calendula or Hypercal solution or a diluted antiseptic preparation. Follow with RICE procedure.
Training	Injury of this type does not usually interfere with normal training.
See your doctor . . .	. . . if there is any sign of infection, increased pain, bleeding continues, if you are feeling ill, or have any new unexplained symptoms.

Frostbite

Skin damage from exposure to sub-freezing temperature, level of injury depending on the temperature and length of exposure.

Signs and symptoms	Numbness, pain, tingling or burning in the injured area, with shivering and some level of skin damage.
Treatment	Medical care should be sought as soon as possible.
Self help	Damaged tissue should never be massaged or rubbed. Remove clothing from damaged areas and immerse them in warm water (the temperature of the water must not be higher than 100F or 37.8C or further injury may result). Drink warm fluids, but avoid all alcohol. After rewarming, cover the affected areas with soft warm clothing. Avoid using the affected limbs until you have received medical care.
See your doctor . . .	. . . in all cases of frostbite, and return if there is any deterioration in the condition or you feel unwell.

Heat illness

Prolonged exposure to hot, humid temperatures during training and racing, can cause a failure of the body's thermostat mechanisms.

Signs and symptoms	*Heatstroke* Rapid heart beat, cramp, dizziness, weakness, and headache. Hot, dry skin (no sweating) with high body temperature. *Heat exhaustion* Low or normal temperature with cool, moist pale skin. Slow pulse, cramp and concentrated urine.

Treatment	It is **essential** that medical aid be sought.
Self help	Cool off. If very hot but not sweating have a cold water shower or bath. If you are sweating and feeling faint, sip cold water or fruit juice. Both conditions are emergencies: arrange for transport to the hospital.
See your doctor . . .	. . . if after being treated at the hospital, you still have symptoms of heatstroke or heat exhaustion. Call immediately! These may be serious or even fatal.

Hyperventilation syndrome

	This condition tends to occur during or following a particularly hard race. Due to the stress of competition or making a supreme effort, your breathing becomes so fast that carbon dioxide levels in the blood are decreased and this temporarily upsets normal blood chemistry.
Signs and symptoms	Rapid breathing with a feeling of severe air hunger. A general feeling of weakness, dry mouth, palpitations, fatigue and sometimes a tendency to faint. Numbness, tingling sensations, muscle spasm or contractions in the hands and feet.
Treatment	Not usually required for this condition, but essential if there is no response to self help.

Self help	At the time of an attack, it is essential to quickly increase the carbon dioxide in the blood to relieve the symptoms.
	    The best way is to cover the mouth and nose completely with a paper bag, breathe slowly into the bag and rebreathe the air in the bag (which contains exhaled carbon dioxide).
	    Breathe slowly in this manner 10 or 15 times, then try to breathe normally for a few minutes.
	    Repeat this process until full recovery is made and the balance is re-established. If you are coping with an attack of hyperventilation in another rider, it helps to keep reassuring the rider that he or she is doing the right thing.

See your doctor . . .	. . . if the symptoms do not diminish with self treatment. If you have repeated attacks and feel that you are prone to hyperventilation, discuss it with your doctor or a sports medicine specialist. At the finish of the 100 kilometre team time trial during the Los Angeles Olympics, one of the British riders showed the symptoms of

hyperventilation. Several onlookers suggested that he should be given oxygen, but we did the paper bag routine and he rapidly recovered.

Ingrowing toenail

The edge of the toenail grows into the flesh of the toe, usually the big toe.

Signs and symptoms

A very painful condition with redness, swelling and heat where the nail pierces the skin.

Treatment

Medical treatment is usually only needed in severe conditions, when a minor operation may be carried out on the toenail.

Self help

The toe should be soaked in warm water containing a mild antiseptic such as Hypercal for about 15 minutes twice a day. Cut a V in the nail to encourage growth and relieve pressure. Lift the corners of the nail and gently insert a small piece of cotton wool under the edges.

See your doctor . . .

. . . if there is increased pain or signs of infection in the toe.

Knee problems

Cycle training takes strength, endurance and stamina, which is strenuous in itself, but racing cyclists seem to all want to push that bit harder – and the knees take the strain. As a result the knee is the most injury-prone of all the joints.

Although racing can cause severe damage to the joint, most problems are caused in training, where the knee is often overused and abused.

Anatomy of the knee and possible sites of injury

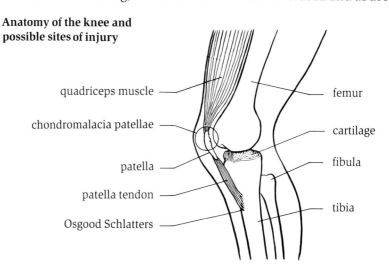

quadriceps muscle —   — femur

chondromalacia patellae —   — cartilage

patella —   — fibula

patella tendon —

Osgood Schlatters —   — tibia

Diagnosis of any joint injury is difficult even for a professional, but the knee can be a particular minefield, do not attempt self diagnosis of any injury to a joint. Any prolonged knee problem should be looked at by a doctor. But before you hit the panic button, it's worth remembering that most of the cycling related knee aches, pains and poppings that a sports therapist sees are not the dreaded cartilage trouble, and sometimes the knee joint is not the problem at all.

Problems can arise from poor position on the bike, incorrectly fitted cleats, and in some cases from the thigh muscles working excessively, especially on cold, wet or windy days. At the end of a hard ride in such conditions, when the quadriceps muscles have been continually contracting and have got gradually tighter, you tend to get minor muscle pulls at the muscle insertions around the knee area. If you use ice massage and quadriceps stretches, the condition often eases in a couple of days. If it persists, then seek qualified help.

Sites of knee bursitis

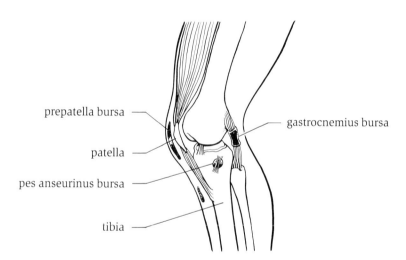

Knee bursitis

Bursas are small fluid-filled sacs or cavities that are designed to prevent friction. They allow muscles and tendons to slip over bones and areas of ligaments. There are many bursas in the knee and any of them may become inflamed through overuse, doing too much too early — the road racing cyclist's 'Easter knee'; as a result of injury, especially falling on the knee; or because of an infection in the knee joint.

Bursitis, as this inflammation is called, can vary in degree from mild irritation to an abcess formation that causes excruciating pain.

Signs and symptoms	Tenderness, swelling, with redness over the affected bursa. Pain on movement and limitation in the movement of the knee.
Treatment	A doctor may prescribe non-steroid anti-inflammatory drugs, a cortisone injection, sometimes mixed with a local anaesthetic or antibiotics according to the condition, and/or pain killers if there is severe pain. Swelling may also call for him to drain some of the fluid. Finally the condition may require an arthroscopic examination, in which a tube is inserted through which the interior of the knee can be looked at, and/or surgery to remove the inflamed bursa.
Self help	RICE for the first 48 hours, then ice massage at least twice a day. After the first 72 hours you may apply heat instead of ice if it feels better. Gentle quads, calf and hamstring stretches are necessary at this stage. The homoeopathic remedy most often used in joint problems is ruta grav. A qualified homoeopath could prescribe a remedy that suits the exact characteristics of your injury.
Training	Training may be resumed once the pain and swelling has been reduced. The progression should be guided by any pain felt. You can always expect some degree of discomfort when restarting training after an injury, and you must learn to discern between discomfort and pain.
See your doctor . . .	. . . if there are any side effects of the prescribed drugs or any sign of infection, increase in pain, or tenderness.
Knee contusion	Bruising of the knee due to a crash or direct blow. Bleeding from damaged blood vessels allows blood to seep into the surrounding soft tissue.
Signs and symptoms	Often skin damage and discoloration along with pain, swelling, tenderness and restricted knee movement. Do not confuse this with *haemarthrosis* (blood in the joint) in which the knee will rapidly swell and become painful and hot. This condition requires immediate medical attention to drain the blood if long term problems are to be avoided.
Treatment	Knee injuries should be treated by your doctor unless the injury is slight.
Self help	RICE for 24 hours, but if still swollen and tender continue for a further

48 hours using an ice pack three or four times a day. After 72 hours you may apply heat instead of ice as it often makes the knee feel easier to use. Use hot packs, showers, heating pads, or embrocations. Massage the thigh above the injury gently to aid circulation and help to decrease the swelling. You could use Lasonil to ease the condition. Arnica ointment 5-10% is a useful application for any closed wound.

Extra vitamin C is always helpful whenever you are dealing with bruises. You can also try supplements of bromelain and papin, the enzymes that digest damaged tissue.

See your doctor . . .   . . . if there is no improvement in the condition in one or two days, or if there are any signs of infection or new unexplained symptoms or side effects to treatments being given.

Knee strain   Injury to the muscles or tendons that attach to bones of the knee. Usually caused by prolonged overuse, sudden fierce effort or subjecting the knee to a level of effort without sufficient preparation, or a crash causing a violent blow or force to the knee.

Signs and symptoms   Muscular spasm, swelling and pain on moving or stretching the knee.

Treatment   Your doctor should make a diagnosis and recommendations for treatment unless the injury is very slight. Your doctor may have prescribed analgesics or anti-inflammatory tablets, or you may wish to use aspirin or paracetamol if the condition is painful.

Self help   RICE as soon as possible, then after medical attention use ice massage three or four times a day for 15 minutes at a time. After 48 hours, apply heat instead of ice, if it feels better. Massage gently above the injury to help ease the discomfort and to decrease the swelling.

Take extra vitamin C. Use one of or a mixture of the essential oils rosemary, lavender and clary sage in a light massage to relax the muscles and ease the pain.

Training   Riding may be resumed once there is pain-free movement; the turbo trainer would be an ideal way to start riding, or flat roads using low gears. Use ice massage for ten minutes before riding.

See your doctor . . .   . . . if pain or swelling worsens despite treatment, or a mild strain fails to improve or persists longer than ten days.

Chondromalacia patellae

Damage to the moving surface of the patella, the kneecap, causing an aching pain behind the kneecap. Pain begins and progresses slowly, tending to occur in individuals between 10-25 years of age. It can be brought on by inbuilt structural problems, but more often is due to our old friend overuse – often by using gears that are too big for your state of fitness or by riding and/or running up hills.

Signs and symptoms

Widespread pain in the knee joint and behind the patella while applying pressure on the pedals. Symptoms are worse after a hard race or hilly training ride. Painful when climbing stairs: the knee 'gives way' at times.

Treatment

A doctor would usually prescribe rest and anti-inflammatory medication or physiotherapy. If there is no improvement in the condition you may be referred to a specialist for arthroscopy, an examination of the inside of the knee to confirm the diagnosis and to remove any degenerative cartilage.

Self help

Although this condition is often diagnosed, our opinion is that it is not as common as we are led to believe. The problem may arise from the patella moving in an abnormal action during the flexion and extension of the knee. There is often no real damage to the inside of the knee and instead what has happened is that overwork has caused the muscles fixing into the knee to shorten or seize up. Sometimes the vastus medialis, the inside thigh muscle, may be slightly weaker, so a visit to the physio may be in order.

Rest is essential; trying to 'ride it out' will only make matters worse.

Apply ice packs for 48 hours then ice massage over the whole of the knee and thigh area followed by gentle stretches to the quadriceps (thigh muscles). Cold limb wraps and/or heat pad treatment can often ease the condition.

If it is possible to have your thigh muscles massaged by a sports therapist it would help to speed things along. If not, self massage with relaxing essential oils such as lavender and rosemary.

Training

Once the pain has subsided you may start to use the turbo trainer or some light riding on the road using low gears. Stay off tracks and rough ground. A good stretching routine, paying extra attention to your thighs and hamstrings, before and after riding, is strongly advised.

Muscle damage

We all experience sore muscles following a longer or harder ride than usual. The action to be taken depends on the degree of discomfort.

If it is mild soreness over the whole of the previously worked muscle area, then probably all you would need to do is cut down on the distance and intensity of your rides. Do light riding on lowish gears, and the problem may resolve itself. If the pain is more intense you might have a muscle strain. This is more serious than sore muscles, as there is greater damage done to the muscle fibres. The localised and persistent pain experienced will indicate to what degree the muscle fibres have been torn.

In cycle sport, muscle strain mainly occurs in the quadricep muscles (thigh muscles). It is not advisable to apply any heat to the injured area for 48 hours. So, no hot soaks in the bath or favourite embrocation creams during the period.

Muscle soreness and strains can have several causes:

* Poor flexibility: lack of correct stretching is a common cause of muscle strains. Read the **Stretching** chapter carefully.

* Poor warm-up: making sudden or intense efforts without having ridden yourself in.

* Overtraining: undertaking a hard training programme which has no adequate rest periods to allow muscle recovery.

* Undertraining: subjecting your muscles to intense effort without prior preparation.

* Mineral deficiency: an electrolyte imbalance can predispose you to muscle strain. (*See* **Minerals** *page 69.*)

* Dehydration: lack of sufficient fluid intake can also lead to muscle strains. (*See* **Fluid Replacement** *page 86.*)

Treatment

To our knowledge there is no medicine currently available that will safely speed up the healing process. The best you can hope for is a prescription to rest, possibly coupled with aspirin or a non-steroidal anti-inflammatory drug from your doctor. As a general rule, the more severe the pain, the greater the injury and the longer the period of recovery.

Self help

RICE or a cold pack as soon as possible for up to 24 hours to the really sore area, followed by some very gentle stretches to the damaged muscle. If the ice irritates the skin, discontinue, but if there is any swelling continue the elevation and or/use a cold water limb wrap.

After 48 hours heat may be applied with a hot water spray, a hot pack or water bottle, heat lamps or pads. Heat will dilate the blood vessels and increase the supply of blood containing nutrients to assist tissue repair. This is a good time to apply a soothing and relaxing mixture of the essential oils lavender, a form of anti-inflammatory, and rosemary (which has natural-pain killing properties) both of which are recommended by aromatherapists for use by sports people.

Extra vitamin C (1g a day) plus antioxidant enzymes can in some cases help speed up recovery. There are specific homoeopathic remedies for muscle strains: arnica soon after the injury followed by rhus tox if the muscle is swollen and hot and is easier when you move it; or ruta grav if there are tendons and ligaments involved.

Homoeopathic arnica oil can be applied in a very light massage.

As an optional extra, take tablets of the digestive enzymes bromelain and papain (available from larger health food shops). These enzymes have the unique ability to digest unhealthy, damaged or diseased tissue and leave healthy tissue untouched.

Training

With a mild to moderate muscle strain, when it's not too painful, you are usually OK to go for gentle rides, which can often help to ease out mild muscle soreness.

Perineal contusion

Crashing and landing on the top tube of the bike causes a direct blow to the floor of the pelvis. Blood from ruptured capillaries seeps into muscles and other soft tissue, causing bruising.

Signs and symptoms

Discolouration, tenderness, pain and swelling in the perineal area.

Treatment

Will require your doctor's attention unless the injury is quite small.

Self help

RICE. Use the ice pack three or four times a day. Using crushed ice or cubes in a plastic bag, wrap the bag in a moist towel and place it over the injury for 20 minutes at a time. After 72 hours you may apply heat instead of ice if it feels better. Use a heat lamp, hot packs, hot shower or heat pads.

See your doctor . . .

. . . if there are signs of infection, any difficulty in passing urine or signs of blood in the urine, or if there is no improvement in the condition despite treatment, or if you have discomfort with sexual intercourse after the condition has healed.

Saddle soreness

This is best avoided by riding in shorts with good quality chamois, which are regularly washed and the chamois subsequently lubricated with products such as Cramer's Skin Lube, Thovaline, Cetavlex or lanolin. This decreases friction between the saddle, the shorts and the sensitive perineum − the area between the legs which bears all the body weight on the saddle.

If you do get saddle soreness, all you can do is rest for a while; apply some Cetavlex or other soothing cream, and wait until the tenderness and redness has disappeared before stepping up your mileage again.

If you have to ride with saddle soreness − maybe at a big event or the final stage of a long race − then use Nupercainal, which is antiseptic and somewhat anaesthetic too. It can also be used over broken skin.

Saddle boils are a nasty problem and may to be treated with an antibiotic cream locally and also tablets from the doctor, but again they can usually be avoided by careful washing of the perineal area with good quality soap or Phisoderm. (*See* **Boils** *page 00.*)

Sinusitis	An inflammation of the mucous membranes of the air-filled cavities in the bones of the head connecting with the nose.
Signs and symptoms	Sinusitis is often linked with a head cold. When the nose infection travels up into the sinuses, it inflames the membranes and causes them to become swollen and create a blockage. This results in pains in the cheekbones, a headache and a thick discharge from the nose.
Treatment	Not usually needed at the start of this condition, but if you are prone to sinus problems, you need to visit your doctor for appropriate medication.
Self help	Cyclists can irritate the membranes of the nose and sinuses by breathing cold and often polluted air. This usually causes an excessive production of mucus, creating the need to clear the nasal passages several times during the training ride or race. Although unsightly it is not a problem and can often be reduced by applying Olbas Oil, Vick or Mentholatum just inside the nose before the ride. Gentle inhalations of steam from hot water with Olbas Oil or Vick added will also help. To fully clear your nose, sniff warm salty water into each nostril and blow out.
Training	Normal training can usually be continued with this condition, unless you have difficulty with breathing or the symptoms increase.
See your doctor . . .	. . . if the condition deteriorates despite self care.
Skin abrasions	Scraped or scratched skin: usually a minor injury, but it can be serious if the skin damage covers a large area or if dirt, gravel, etc., has become imbedded in it due to bad primary care.

Signs and symptoms   Skin scraped or irritated usually with some bleeding. Some immediate pain may be experienced, but this is often of short duration.

Treatment   Medical attention is not usually required for minor injuries, but a doctor may need to give treatment for more extensive or infected abrasions, or if something is deeply imbedded in the wound.

Self help   If you fall off your bike you usually get a lot of grazing, 'gravel rash', 'track burns' and so on. Clean it up with soap and water. The least painful way to do this is to put the dilute antiseptic in a clean garden spray-type bottle and then spray over the damaged area: the force of the solution applied will dislodge any imbedded grit. Our homoeopathic alternative antiseptic is a solution of hypericum and calendula (available as Hypercal tincture in health food shops and some pharmacies). Diluted witch-hazel is also useful to stop bleeding and promote healing.

The usual scrape or scratch only needs to be washed with plain soap and water as soon as possible. A good time to do this is when you shower after a race or training session. Some slight grazes don't even need a dressing, in fact they can often heal quicker exposed to fresh air. If the wound is more serious, then it will need a dressing, applied either dry or with a proprietary antiseptic cream or homoeopathic ointment. Calendula is a good homoeopathic preparation to apply; it is not antiseptic, but it is aseptic and inhibits bacterial growth.

If the wound becomes infected, then usually you have not given it the care it required, and you must visit your doctor who may want to prescribe antibiotics. You must be a little cautious regarding the skin with the use of antibiotics because in some people they can cause increased sensitivity, creating a new problem rather than solving an old one.

If skin damage is due to friction, protect the area against further abrasion by the use of gauze or moleskin.

Check and cleanse every day. If crusting forms too early and limits movement, or oozing occurs, soak in warm water containing mild antiseptic water or Hypercal lotion. To prevent infection keep the wound clean and keep re-applying a tincture or ointment until it is improved.

Cover lightly with a bandage while riding during the day but leave the wound open to air while resting at home.

For minor pain or discomfort, use soluble aspirin or paracetamol, although if arnica has been given this should not be needed; although it has no analgesic action of its own with its ability to rapidly heal damaged tissue and blood vessels it has the effect of easing pain.

See your doctor . . . . . . if it is too painful for you to clean all debris from the injury, or any signs of infection or unexplained symptoms develop.

Skin laceration

Lacerations in bike riding are usually the result of a crash creating a combination injury of a bruised, jagged, irregular cut.

Treatment A deep or long cut will need to be cleaned and stitched up by a doctor, using a local anaesthetic, so you may need to go to the hospital for help. The doctor may also decide to prevent the possibility of tetanus by giving a booster dose of tetanus toxoid.

Keep the wound covered with a bandage and if it gets wet, replace it. If bleeding occurs after stitching, control it by applying firm pressure to the wound for about 10 minutes; if the bleeding continues, return to the doctor or hospital.

Self help If there is profuse bleeding, cover the injured area with a cloth and apply pressure directly to the laceration for 10 minutes to stem the bleeding. If it is a large gash don't waste time waiting to see if it is going to stop bleeding, go and get it stitched up properly by a doctor. Use only firm pressure: do not use a tourniquet.

For an injury with light bleeding: clean the wound carefully with water and Hypercal solution, hold edges of cut together, apply gauze dressing. Cleaning with diluted witch-hazel will also help to control the bleeding.

Tea tree or eucalyptus oil is reputed to be a natural antiseptic essential oil that can be applied. Lavender oil applied several times a day can help the cuts to heal quickly.

In the event of pain or discomfort you may take paracetamol; do not use aspirin as it can increase the possibility of bleeding.

See your doctor . . . . . . if the wound should develop any sign of infection.

Sunburn

Sunburn is a regular problem for cyclists due to the distances covered in racing and training, often leading to hours of exposure to the sun.
The depth of damage is classed as follows:
First degree burn − mild redness.
Second degree burn − redness and sometimes blisters.
Third degree burn − redness, blisters and severe skin damage.

Signs and symptoms	Painful, red, blistered and sometimes ulcerated skin. Severe burns may bring on chills, fever, nausea and vomiting.
Treatment	Essential in all cases of severe sunburn. Aspirin or paracetamol may be required to relieve the pain. Other medication or skin applications should have the approval of the doctor in case of any severe reaction due to skin sensitivity. During the Falklands war Flammazine cream was used with amazing success and may be prescribed by your doctor.
Self help	Where possible, immerse the sunburnt limb in cold water for ten minutes to reduce the heat and pain. Failing this, soak towels in cold water and gently apply to the burn.

After cold water, apply a liberal smearing of concentrated vitamin E oil, (from a punctured capsule) which will encourage healing and prevent scars forming. Repeat every two hours. Take 800 μ of vitamin E and 1g of vitamin C a day while healing is going on.

Success in the treatment of burns is claimed for the essential oil of lavender. It is a natural painkiller as well as being an antiseptic and can be applied neat or soaked into a gauze bandage.

Prevention	Always apply a good sunblock preparation with protection against both UV-A and UV-B rays before long rides in the sun.
See your doctor . . .	. . . if the condition does not improve following medical attention, or if you have a high body temperature, sickness or diarrhoea.

Tendon damage   Tendons are strong, inelastic, fibrous bands that attach muscles to bone. Muscles and tendons are an integral unit working as one, although of differing tissue density.

Exercise contracts the muscle fibres and in some cases the muscle fibres stay shortened, creating greater stress to the tendinous tissue and making it more prone to injury throughout the length of the tendon.

Achilles tendinitis (inflammation of the Achilles tendon)   Achilles tendon damage can be caused by pressure on the tendon from new, high back, cycling shoes, strain from overuse of the lower leg muscles and Achilles tendon, or by infection following an injury.

Signs and symptoms   Constant pain or pain with movement. Heat and redness over the inflamed Achilles tendon. Limited range of movement of the ankle often with a crackling sound when the tendon moves.

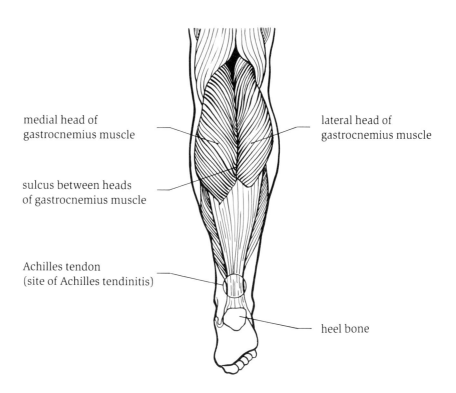

medial head of
gastrocnemius muscle

lateral head of
gastrocnemius muscle

sulcus between heads
of gastrocnemius muscle

Achilles tendon
(site of Achilles tendinitis)

heel bone

Treatment	Doctor's examination, diagnosis and anti-inflammatory medication or treatment with ultra-sound if required.
Self help	Ice massage over the whole of the calf muscle and tendon area, followed with some gentle calf stretches. The homoeopathic remedy ruta grav is helpful where tendons are involved, and this is available in a cream which you can rub gently into the tendon, as well as in tablets to take.
Training	If the condition was caused by new shoes, use your old ones until you are fully recovered. Do not race for about ten days, with only light riding while it is still inflamed. Reassess after ten days.
See your doctor . . .	. . . if the condition does not improve, or side effects or unexplained symptoms develop.
Thigh strain	Injury to the muscles and/or tendons of the thigh. Chronic strains are caused by overuse; acute strains by overstress or direct injury.

Strains are graded into three types:

Grade 1 – Mild – slight muscle strain with only micro tearing of muscle fibres with no loss of strength.

Grade 2 – Moderate – with tearing of muscle or tendinous fibres causing diminished strength.

Grade 3 – Severe – rupture of the muscle-tendon-bone attachment with separation of fibres. A severe strain often requires surgery.

Signs and symptoms

Muscle spasm, swelling and pain when moving or stretching the hip or knee. Inflammation of sheath covering a tendon in the thigh. Loss of muscle strength.

Treatment

A doctor's diagnosis is required for moderate or severe strains, in case surgery is needed.

Self help

RICE for 48 hours, then use heat or ice massage three or four times a day for not longer than ten minutes at a time.

In painful cases you may take Nurofen and massage the injured thigh gently to provide comfort and decrease swelling, wrapping with an elasticized bandage between treatments. Use arnica oil if it is the result of a direct injury; rosemary and lavender oils if brought on by overuse. A cold water limb wrap may also be applied.

Training

Light riding without pain on the turbo trainer or flat local roads; apply ice massage for ten minutes before riding.

See your doctor . . .

. . . if pain or swelling worsens despite treatment, or a mild strain does not improve or persists for longer than ten days.

Stocking your own first aid kit

Getting to injuries and minor problems while they are 'fresh' can make all the difference between a quick recovery and serious 'down time'. Trained people are not always on hand to deal with injuries, so it makes sense to be personally well prepared.

Start your kit with a few essentials in a container with plenty of room – you'll be bound to keep adding to it.

FIRST AID KIT

Cold pack

You can buy several types of cold packs from chemists. We prefer the crystal dry pack, as it requires no attention until you need it. Then all you do is give the pack a firm blow, which will break the vial inside, and mix the crystals with its contents: the pack will become cold.

Bandages

Keep a selection of various sizes of elastic and tubular bandages. Use to hold dressings in place, or to use for compression.

Adhesive tape

Useful to hold dressings in place or for fixing ends of bandages. Avoid zinc oxide tape if your skin is sensitive to it.

Safety pins

Keep a few in various sizes, as they are useful in many situations.

Dressings

A selection of dry gauze and non-stick dressings in sterile packs. Antiseptic soap and water is probably as good as anything for cleaning wounds, but if you prefer an antiseptic cream, Savlon is good.

Scissors

Blunt ended are safer to use.

Tweezers

For removing splinters etc.

Nail clippers

A good pair of nail clippers is an investment. They make trimming nails easier.

Moleskin and plasters

For skin protection and small cuts.

Medications

Arnica, Hypercal tincture, calendula ointment, essential oils, Paracetamol or soluble aspirin as a painkiller and anti-inflammatory if you are not sensitive to them.

8   Health and fitness

Health and fitness do not always go together; both have to be worked at. Some cyclists train in a dedicated manner all year, but end up with disappointing results because they neglect their health, hygiene, and diet. You must aim for a high standard of personal health if you hope to get any success. Here are the bare essentials.

1.   Do not take good health for granted: keeping healthy is as much a part of your training as getting out on the bike.
2.   During the winter months, and well before race training starts in earnest, check the following:
   a   Visit the dentist and have any problems dealt with. Have composite fillings rather than mercury amalgam if possible.
   b   Try to arrange for a medical examination (heart, lungs, urine, blood). This may be difficult to get and you may have to pay.
   c   Have a full course of anti-tetanus injections.
3.   Develop the following general practices of personal hygiene:
   a   Wear your hair reasonably short, or tied back, so that it is easier to look after. Flowing or bushy hair will increase wind drag.
   b   Keep your finger-nails short − and clean.
   c   Brush your teeth every day without fail − work on preventing decay, for if your teeth are infected you could develop problems in other areas of the body.
   d   Take a bath or shower frequently − daily if possible, but always after prolonged effort such as a race, or a circuit training or weight training session.
   e   Always, **without fail**, wash the crotch area after any riding. Neglect could result in a prolonged, painful time off the bike.
   f   Always wash your hands after visiting the lavatory.
   g   Give special attention to your feet: they should be washed daily. Cut the nails straight across to help prevent ingrowth. Socks worn one day, or for one period, should not be put on again until they've been washed. Wear clean socks every day and after every hard working period such as a training session or race.

   h Change underclothes as frequently as convenient: preferably daily, and always after exercise, training or racing.

   i Try to avoid wearing the same racing clothes without their being washed. They retain sweat, which harbours infective bacteria. This applies especially to the chamois inserts in shorts. Wash them carefully, rinse very thoroughly and − if the insert is real chamois − dry slowly, never in front of a fire or on a radiator.

4 After finishing an event, do not stand about in scanty and sweat-soaked clothes. Wash, or rub down with a towel, perhaps with eau-de-cologne, and put on clean, dry clothes. Put on your track suit at once, whatever the weather conditions.

5 Shoes as well as socks can absorb a great deal of sweat. They should be cleaned inside, otherwise they become dangerously infectious as well as unpleasantly odorous. The best remedy is to use a disinfectant. If possible, have two pairs of shoes so you can use them on alternate days.

6 Try to ensure that you regularly have sufficient sleep. There is no general period necessary for everyone. Some need much more, some much less than others. A week's trial of no alarm, no call, but just waking naturally (and getting up at once) would show your needs.

REMINDERS

1 Have a medical check-up.

2 Have a dental check-up.

3 Have a full course of anti-tetanus treatment. Remember that you need a booster every five years. Carry your card to races or you will be given another dose in the event of a crash.

4 Start having early nights.

5 Cut out highly spiced foods.

6 Remember always to take food out training; your body uses up calories to keep warm.

7 Take a multi-vitamin tablet (at least) every day.

8 Train thoroughly and hard **no playing about**.

9 Do not slip-stream behind other traffic when training.

10 Shower or rub down as soon as you get home.

Sex and racing

Yes, they do mix! The fitter you are, the higher your energy and the better your sexual functions are likely to be. If you are unfit, you may be unable to perform the sexual act as well as you would otherwise.

Sex before racing – the night before – poses no problems providing that sex occupies a regular part of your life. If you are used to regular sex, then abstaining just because of a race the following day will do you no good at all. If you don't have a regular sexual relationship, then it is a different story: the hours of sleep lost when out looking for sex are just as detrimental as the 'effort' itself.

Travelling positively   If you are going to be any good at cycle racing, you can expect at some point to be invited to race abroad. Travel can adversely affect performance, especially when it involves the disorientation caused by changing time zones. So it is in your interests to try to minimise the disruption of travelling, especially to somewhere new, in as many ways as possible.

Start by learning about the country concerned: the climate, the terrain, the local food and customs. If you know what differences to expect, then you are better prepared for any stress when trying to adapt.

Jet lag can also cause problems; it upsets your body rhythms, your biological clock and probably your digestion. You wake up and go to sleep at the wrong time. Unless you have plenty of time to adapt, your body will not function efficiently.

Minimising the effects of jet lag is achieved by a few easy precautions. First of all, don't try to get in a lot of miles immediately before departure, so that you don't start the trip in an exhausted state. A missed day of training is a small price to pay for arriving in a much better condition. When you get on the plane, adjust your watch to the local time of your destination. In this way you are already starting to adjust to the new venue. Think of your day and night patterns immediately in terms of your destination. As far as you can, start to eat and sleep as if you were already in the new time zone.

When eating, remember that for the first half of the day you should be having more protein, and in the second half you should have more carbohydrate. On the plane, if it is breakfast time at your destination, select items which have more protein, then as the day goes on adjust to take in more carbohydrate. Don't eat a lot, but drink plenty of non-alcoholic fluids.

If you are in for a long journey, try to sleep on the plane. Take some slippers, and wear loose clothing so your circulation is unrestricted. Have a walk around the cabin from time to time to give your heart some work, or do some easy isometric exercises in your seat.

Physiological changes take place when flying that also contribute to jet lag. These are caused by the pressurised, air-conditioned environment and the fact that flying lifts us out of the dense, protective layer of the earth's atmosphere, so air travellers are more exposed to radiation from the sun. All this helps to cause an over-production of cell-damaging substances known as free radicals. You can help nullify the effects of jet lag by topping up your body's supply of antioxidant vitamins and minerals, such as vitamins C, A and E, and the minerals selenium and zinc.

When you arrive, go for a gentle ride to assess the conditions and get your bearings. If you are at the world championships, for instance, don't get caught up in a fast-moving training group of international stars if you visit the course. Far better to gently reconnoitre the course at your own pace, and to concentrate on recovering from the journey.

Extreme conditions

It would be nice if all racing and training were carried out in ideal conditions, but we don't live in an ideal world. So you need to know what precautions to take in extremes of weather.

Hot weather

One of the biggest problems of just being in a hot country is dehydration. We ususally eat and drink to a set pattern and don't take into consideration the increase in temperature and the body's requirment for more fluid. Drink plenty of fluids – water, fruit juice or electrolyte replacement drinks – anything to replace the loss in sweat. Avoid foods that are going to push up your body temperature, particularly chocolate. Don't take salt tablets except under medical supervision.

Clothing should be loose-fitting to allow the air to flow through, and you should protect your neck and the tender parts of the upper arms with sun-barrier cream. If you don't have a sun-tan and come to race in a hot climate, then use a barrier cream with the appropriate strength factor. Check that it's a cream that protects both from UV-A and UV-B radiation, or you run the risk of damage to deeper layers of the skin without feeling yourself burn. You will need protective headgear when racing, of course, but be sure to wear a hat at all times in strong sunlight.

Dehydration is the major danger, closely followed by heat exhaustion. Signs of this are dizziness, headache and lack of co-ordination. If you notice these symptoms, get off your bike and sit in the shade until help arrives.

Cold weather

A warm drink at the right time is a great advantage and the colder the conditions the more important the cold drink becomes. You can take warm foods and drinks in a thermos flask which fits your bottle cage, or in a thermic bottle, or in a thermos refill fitted into the bottom half of a normal feeding bottle.

You need to eat more because of the extra calories used in actually keeping warm. So the proverbial Mars or Hershie bar is an important part of your diet!

Just because you are racing, it doesn't mean that you should be in a short-sleeved jersey and skin shorts whatever the temperature. If it is cold, don't hesitate to wear training tights, extra jerseys, gloves, hat and overshoes. You can also put warming embrocation on the knees – an oil-based one if the conditions are wet.

In cold conditions be alert to the danger signs of numbness and shivering, and a tightening of the stomach. Frostbite in the fingers is not totally unknown. If you suspect you might have frostbite, then restore warmth to the threatened fingers or toes very gradually. Do not rub them and make for the hospital as soon as possible. (*See* **What to do for frostbite**, *page 114*.)

High altitude

If you go straight into racing at high altitude without being acclimatised first it can be a traumatic experience, because the body's ability to breathe normally is impaired. You need a period of at least three weeks training to acclimatise properly. A high dosage of vitamin E – about 1000mg daily – can be helpful but only under close supervision.

Another problem associated with altitude is dehydration, so look once more to your fluid intake and your pulse rate, which will go very high at first. Again this can be countered with 200mg of vitamin E daily until your pulse stabilises, then move up to the higher dosage.

If you are taking medication, especially sleeping tablets, watch for increased effectiveness and dose accordingly.

Acquired immune deficiency syndrome (AIDS)

Being diagnosed HIV-positive, or developing some of the signs of 'full blown' AIDS, does not mean you have to give up cycling. Far from it: the aerobic exercise of cycling strengthens the heart and circulation, which helps stimulate the thymus gland, an important part of the immune system. In addition, the benefits of cycling that most people tend to take for granted assume a greater importance for someone who needs extra help to stay healthy – fresh air, exposure to natural daylight and the healthy elimination of toxins through sweating, for instance.

That said, a key part of living with HIV and/or AIDs is to reduce mental, emotional and physical stress. So that means it is even more important to listen to your body and recognise when you might be pushing it too far.

The diagnosis of HIV infection is not a death sentence. Even the most entrenched scientific opinion now seems to agree that HIV is only one of a number of possible co-factors involved in the development of AIDS.

Evidence from the longest-running AIDS research project, based in San Francisco, shows men with HIV infection who have not developed AIDS for up to 12 years after infection. This is not to minimise the fact that HIV infection means that those infected have a high risk of developing AIDS, and all possible means to stop the transmission of HIV should be used.

When the immune system is busy coping with HIV, the body is less able to handle normal run-of-the-mill viruses and bacteria, so you must preserve energy: do not over-tire yourself, make sure you rest after exercise, and take in good quality food and supplements. It will be important to make sure that calories expended in riding your bike are replaced, but do this with nutrient-rich foods, not sugary snacks and drinks, which will not help the immune system.

As yet there is no way of reversing the effects of AIDS, but regular exercise is one part of a programme to strengthen your immune system.

Preventing cancer

The human body is made up of millions of cells, of many different types. Although they look and work differently, they repair and reproduce in much the same way. Our cells die off naturally and are continually replaced by new cells, reproduced through cell division. This normally takes place in an orderly and controlled manner, but if they are affected by cancer, they get out of control, growing and dividing unnecessarily, forming a lump of new tissue – what is known as a tumour.

Tumours can either be benign or malignant. A benign tumour is not regarded as cancerous as the cells do not spread to other parts of the body. The problem with a benign tumour is that if the cells continue to multiply, the tumour could start to crowd out an organ or interfere with a vital part or function of the body. A malignant tumour *is* cancerous, and consists of cells which have the ability to spread. If unchecked – either naturally by the immune system or by treatment – it will often spread into the surrounding tissues or even break away from the original site, being transported by the bloodstream or lymphatic system to create tumours in other parts of the body.

Cancer is not one disease with a single cause and a single type of treatment. If it was, it might not pose such a problem to medical science, but there are over 200 different kinds. In the two forms discussed here, spreading via the bloodstream or lymphatic system is uncommon providing the cancer is treated.

Skin cancer

One of the great pleasures of cycling is the time that we can spend in the sunshine and fresh air. Regretfully, that can also be a mark against it, because research now suggests that spending long periods in strong sunlight can be one of the principle causes of skin cancer.

Don't take fright and rush off to sell your bike, though: prevention is thought possible. If we give you some information on the disease that no one wants to talk about, you will be able to take some preventive measures or recognise the signs and symptoms and get an early diagnosis − which increases your options for treatment.

What causes skin cancer?

Excessive exposure to the ultraviolet rays of the sun is the main cause of skin cancers, which appear to be on the increase. Holes in the ozone layer have been blamed for the increase, since these are undeniably letting through more of the sun's damaging radiation. But it is also possible that this increased exposure has come about because of the increase in leisure time − more of us are able to get outdoors and travel to hotter countries for our holidays.

Most of us at some time have envied the bronzed look of Tour de France riders, for we tend to regard a suntan as healthy and attractive, and brown legs make us feel fit even when we're not. But the time these riders spend in the strong sun can increase the risk of skin cancer if they − and even we − do not use proper skin protection. Use cream or oils with a high protection factor, and a total sun-block on sensitive areas like your nose − one of the first places to get burned.

Scientists have estimated that three-quarters of our total lifetime dose of ultraviolet radiation is accumulated before the age of 20. This early dose is important, because one theory of the development of skin cancers says that it is brought about by a build-up of over-exposure to the sun over a period of several years. Youngsters who have had excessive exposure to the sun run an increased risk of developing some form of skin cancer later on in life − often not until they are in their 60s or 70s.

The two most common types of skin cancer are basal cell and squamous cell carcinomas. They rarely spread to other parts of the body and are usually cured with modern treatment techniques.

People from black or dark-skinned races rarely develop skin cancer because the melanin pigment in their skin gives them a level of protection. Fair-skinned people who tend to burn are most at risk.

Testicular cancer

Testicular cancer was at one time a common cause of death in young men aged 25 to 35. Thankfully that has now changed, for with improved treatment and early diagnosis there is every chance of it being cured.

Young men are rarely, if ever, told anything about about the risk of testicular cancer. From the age of 15 upwards young men should be aware of the need to examine their testicles every month for any variation from the norm. What you are looking for is any swelling within the testicle or a hard lump with a feeling of pressure, or discomfort in the lower abdomen or testicle. Although there may be some discomfort, it is not so in every case, and very rarely is there any great pain. So you can see how easy it is to shrug off the lumps as normal, delaying the detection of the cancer.

Self-examination is a simple procedure and is best carried out while having a shower or bath, when the testicles tend to be hanging more loosely from the body. A normal testicle is egg-shaped with a spongy, firm consistency. Both testicles should be carefully examined by rolling gently between the thumb and first two fingers, one at a time. If during the self-examination you find that the testicle is misshapen or you feel an unusual growth, you must seek medical advice. Early detection is vital: the earlier the detection, the greater the chance of a complete cure.

BACUP produce several information leaflets on cancers of all types; they are worth getting to become more knowledgeable on the subject, and possibly put your mind at rest. (*See* **Useful Addresses** *page 142.*)

Doping control in sport

Banned substances and practices

This list is issued by the Medical Commission of the UCI. It is based on that issued by the International Olympic Committee, but is not completely identical.

Section 1:
Doping classes

a. *Stimulants, e.g.*

amphenazole	ephedrine	morazone
amphepramone	etafedrine	nikethamide
amphetamine	ethamivan	pemoline
amphetaminil	ethylamphetamine	pentetrazol
benzphetamine	fencamfamin	phendimetrazine
caffeine*	fenetylline	phenmetrazine
chlorphentermine	fenproporex	phentermine
clobenzorex	furfenorex	phenylpropanolamine
clorprenaline	meclofenoxate	pipradol
cocaine	mefenorex	prolintane
cropropamide	methoxyphenamine	propylhexedrine
crotetamide	methylamphetamine	pyrovalerone
diethylpropion	methylephedrine	strychnine
dimetamfetamine	methylphenidate	*and related compounds.*

*For caffeine, the definition of a positive depends upon the following: if the concentration in urine exceeds 12 micrograms/ml.

b. *Narcotic analgesics, e.g.*

anileridine	diamorphine (heroin)	pentazocine
buprenorphine	dihydrocodeine	pethidine
codeine	dipipanone	phenazocine
dextromoramide	methadone	trimeperidine
dextropropoxyphen	morphine	*and related compounds.*

c. *Anabolic steroids, e.g.*

bolasterone	nandrolone
boldenone	norethandrolone
chlordehydromethyltestosterone	oxnadrolone
clostebol	oxymesterone
fluoxymesterone	oxymetholone
mesterolene	stanozolol
methandienone	testosterone**
methenolone	*and related compounds.*
methyltestosterone	

**For testosterone, the definition of a positive depends upon the following: the administration or the use of any other manipulation having the result of increasing the ratio in urine of testosterone /epitestosterone to above 6.

d. *Peptide hormones and analogues, e.g.*
Chorionic gonadotrophin (HCG – human chorionic gonadotrophin):
It is well known that the administration to males of HCG and other compounds with related activity leads to an increased rate of production of endogenous androgenic steroids and is considered equivalent to exogenous administration of testosterone.

Corticotrophin (ACTH):
Corticotrophin has been misused to increase the blood levels of endogenous corticosteriods, notably to obtain the euphoric effect of corticosteroids. The application of corticotrophin is considered to be equivalent to the oral, intra-muscular or intravenous application of corticosteroids.

Growth hormone (HGH Somatotrophin):
The misuse of growth hormone in sport is deemed to be unethical and dangerous because of various adverse effects, for example allergic reactions, and acromegaly when applied in high doses.

All the respective releasing factors of the above mentioned substances are also banned.

Section 2:
Methods

1. Blood doping
Blood doping is forbidden

2. Pharmacological, chemical and physical manipulation
The BCF and the UCI ban the use of substances and methods which alter the integrity and validity of urine samples used in doping controls. Examples of banned methods are catheterisation, urine substitution and/or tampering, inhibition or renal excretion e.g. by probenecid and related compounds.

Section 3:
Classes of drugs
subject to certain
restrictions

1. Local anaesthetics
Injectable local anaesthetics are permitted under the following conditions:
i. that procaine, xylocaine and carbocaine, etc., are used but not cocaine
ii. only local or intra-articular may be administered
iii.only when medically justified.

2. Corticosteroids
The use of corticosteroids is banned except for topical use (aural, ophthalmological and dermatological), inhalational therapy (asthma, allergic rhinitis) and local or intra-articular injections.

BCF treatment
guidelines

Examples of permitted and prohibited substances (based upon International Olympic Committee Doping Classes):

Asthma
Allowed: Terbutaline, Salbutamol, Ventolin, Intal, Becotide.
(*NB* Inhalers only.)

Cough
Allowed: steam and menthol inhalations, Benylin expectorant.
All antibiotics.
Banned: products containing codeine, ephedrines.

Diarrhoea
Allowed: Dioralyte, Lomotil, Motilum.
Banned: products containing codeine or morphine.

Hayfever
Allowed: antihistamines, Triludan, Piriton, Histryll, Beconase, Otrivine, Opticrom eye drops.
Banned: products containing ephedrine, pseudoephedrine.

Headache
Allowed: Paracetamol, Aspirin, Anadin.
Banned: products containing codeine, dextropropoxyphene.

Sore throat
Allowed: soluble paracetamol gargle.

Vomiting
Allowed: Dioralyte, Rehidrat, Maxolon.

Warning
Some herbal preparations may contain banned substances naturally occurring in plants. If taken, they may bring about a positive finding of a banned substance. Presently there is no requirement for a comprehensive listing of ingredients in nutritional supplements. It is advisable to avoid products containing the plant Ma Huang (Chinese Ephedra) as this plant contains the stimulant substance ephedrine. Commercial ginseng preparations may also contain substitute or additional substances.

   The above are only examples of substances currently permitted or prohibited. If in doubt check with your governing body or the Sports Council (071 388 1277). Remember − you are responsible. Information supplied by The Sports Council. Reproduced with permission.

Further reading

Useful addresses

1 Daniel D. Arnheim, *Modern Principles of Athletic Training*, Times Mirror/Mosby College Publishing, St Louis, Missouri: 1989

2 Gertrude Beard and Elizabeth C. Wood, *Massage: Principles and Techniques*, W. B. Saunders, London: 1974

3 Fellowship of Sports Masseurs and Therapists, *Sports Therapy Course Notes*: 1985

4 H. Winter Griffith MD, *Complete Guide to Sports Injuries*, Body Press, Los Angeles: 1986

5 Lyle W. Morgan II, *Treating Sports Injuries the Natural Way*, Thorsons Publishing Group, Wellingborough: 1990

6 Rob Sleamaker, *Serious Training for Serious Athletes*, Leisure Press, Champaign, Illinois: 1989

7 Frank Westell and Ken Evans, *Cycle Racing (revised edition)*, Springfield Books, Huddersfield: 1991

Fellowship of Sports Masseurs and Therapists, B. M. Soigneur, London WC1N 3XX
tel: 081 886 3120

British Cycling Federation, 36 Rochingham Road, Kettering, Northants NN16 8HG
tel: 0536 412211

NutriTec (Enzymes), 17 Pershore Road, South Birmingham B30 3EE tel: 021 433 4001

Cycling Weekly, IPC Magazines Ltd, Kings Reach Tower, Stamford Street, London SE1 9LS tel: 071 261 5588

London Sports Medicine Institute, Medical College of St Bartholomews Hospital, Charterhouse Square, London EC1M 6BC
tel: 071 251 0583

Sports Council, 16 Upper Woburn Place, London WC1H 0QP tel: 071 388 1277

BACUP (Cancer Advice), 121 – 123 Charterhouse Street, London WC1M 6AA tel: 071 608 1661

A Nelson & Co Ltd (Homoeopathic Supplies), 5 Endeavour Way, London SW19
tel: 081 946 8527

Index